Falling into My Place

God Has a Plan for Your Life— Lessons from the Snowflake

D1607459

PAM WILSON

CROSSBOOKS

CrossBooks™
A Division of LifeWay
1663 Liberty Drive
Bloomington, IN 47403
www.crossbooks.com
Phone: 1-866-879-0502

First published by CrossBooks 05/16/2013

ISBN: 978-1-4627-2770-4 (sc)
ISBN: 978-1-4627-2771-1 (e)

Printed in the United States of America.

This book is printed on acid-free paper.

DEDICATION

Falling Into My Place is dedicated to the people God has placed in my life.

God has truly blessed me with parents, grandparents, and even aunts and uncles who prayed for me and modeled the life of a Godly adult.

I am thankful for teachers like Miss Iseminger, our 7th grade English teacher at Altoona High School, who gave me a chance to read my stories in front of her class. She inspired her students to enjoy the wonderful, world of words.

For all my former students, especially my first grade students at Des Moines Christian School, it was a pleasure to help you learn your a-b-c's and 1-2-3's. The amazing things that you did and said in Room 150 will never be forgotten. The teachers, principals, and Dr. Bob Stouffer were my mentors and friends.

A big thank you has to go to my husband. He has been blessed with the gift of generosity and has always encouraged me in my endeavors, no matter the cost.

Our children have given us pages of stories regarding their own talents and skills. It is so rewarding for us to see what God is doing in their lives and in the lives of their families.

He has used all of these people, and many others along the way, to help me find my own special place in life.

TABLE OF CONTENTS

INTRODUCTION

It is the long anticipated, first snowfall day. Beautiful, white, fluffy flakes of snow are falling from the sky outside our classroom window.

I stand at the front of the room before my class. A pair of scissors and a square of white paper are in my hand.

I begin to fold the paper as I have done for many years for hundreds of students.

Cute, little people all over the room are wondering what their teacher is doing as she takes the scissors and snips tiny cuts into the folded paper.

I place the scissors on my desk and begin, ever so gently and ever so slowly, to unfold the square of white paper and hold it up high into the air.

These 25 delightful, first grade children are just beginning their journey on the educational trail, and I ask them, "What is this?"

And they joyfully reply, "A snowflake!"

"You, my dearest students, are a lot like this snowflake. There are no two snowflakes exactly alike. Each one of you is unique. You are wonderfully made by our Heavenly Father!"

Psalm 136:1 "We are fearfully and wonderfully made . . ."

"You are a treasure just waiting to be examined! And I can hardly wait to see what you will do and what you will become.

Look out the window at the beautiful snowflakes. They are all gently falling into place."

This book was written to help you find that special place of service that God has for you. May it give you great joy as you begin to see God's wonderful plan for you and those you love "Falling Into Place."

CHAPTER ONE

"So You Think You Know Your Snowflakes"

Every snowflake has its own unique shape and is different than all other snowflakes. We have all heard that lesson many times.

Every winter my students loved to see those white, fluffy flakes falling from the sky just outside our classroom windows.

January was always a great time to cut out snowflakes and put them up on the bulletin board.

Our class would also use a special kind of graphic organizer called a Venn diagram to help the students make comparisons.

Sometimes the children would choose to compare snowflakes and people. So I would make a diagram on the whiteboard like the one on the following page and wait for students to come up with ideas.

Snowflake ideas would go in the left oval. Ideas about people would go in the right oval. Ideas that pertained to both were put in the middle.

Venn Diagram

Snowflakes	Both	People
Cold Non-Living Don't need food Melt	Sparkle Symmetrical Arrive in different Colors No Two Alike May change under Pressure Made by God Have Purpose Beautiful	Warm Living Need Food Die

Venn Diagram Comparison

Many of the thoughts that came from that comparison activity are found in this book. They led me to do more research about snowflakes.

Snowflakes and human beings are wonderful works of God. No two people are exactly alike. No two snowflakes are exactly alike. People and snowflakes are similar in several ways.

God created people with many different and significant intelligences and He has placed each one of us into our families in a special order. These attributes help to determine the plan that God has for our lives.

Lets begin with a brief look at some snowflake information.

Snowflakes are easily recognized by their hexagonal shape and are also symmetrical.

Like snowflakes, we human beings have a certain recognizable shape and appear to be symmetrical.

However, when we give a closer look, we realize that such is not the case. For example, we have a right foot that is a little bigger than our left. That is why it is a good idea to always try on the right shoe first when looking for footwear. Careful study of snowflake photographs also indicates some differences.

Here are some other interesting discoveries.

Like people, snowflakes aren't always white. We both arrive on this planet in a variety of colors.

Many years ago coal was used in homes and factories. Then the snow was often gray because the coal dust went into the air and was absorbed by the clouds.

In areas such as Prince Edward Island, Canada, where the soil is red clay, snowflakes often look pink. The red dust from the soil is blown into the air and absorbed by the clouds.

Snowflakes and people come in different sizes.

The largest snowflakes ever recorded fell in the state of Montana. Snowflakes that fell on that particular day were 15 inches in diameter.

There are also some interesting similarities regarding where snowflakes and people seem to fall or gather. (Population)

There are places on earth where human beings do not live. It may be too hot or too cold.

Sometimes there are only a few people living in a certain area. Yet, in large cities, there are often many people living in the radius of just a mile.

Some places on earth never see a snowflake, some get just a few flakes, and some are inundated with many feet of the fluffy stuff.

In the state of Washington, at Stampede Pass, the average snowfall is 430 inches a year. And we thought we got a lot of snow in Iowa! That's a lot of snow!

Other snowflake information:

- The average snowflake falls at a speed of 3.1 miles per hour.
- "Snirt" is dirty snow that flies off the dusty prairies in Canada.
- Billions of snowflakes fall during one short snowstorm.
- Snowflakes are made up of ice crystals

Pressure Influences Snowflake Size and Shape

The pressure they receive from the weight of other snow crystals influences the size and shape of snowflakes.

Just like snowflakes, what we become and do with our lives is sometimes influenced by pressure from those around us. Our parents, grandparents, friends and acquaintances often make a big impact on our important life decisions.

Snowflakes are Made Up of Snow Crystals

Every snowflake is a collection of snow crystals.

So, too, we human beings are a collection of our genetic backgrounds. This is our human heritage.

Snowflakes Change With Age

Every snowflake changes as it ages and this changing snow is called "Metamorphosed Snow".

As people age, they also change. Our appearance as well as our personality can change with time. Gray hair and wrinkles appear. Daily wear and tear on our bodies takes a toll on knees, hips, hearts, brains, and various other parts of our bodies.

No Two Snowflakes Are Exactly Alike

Human fingerprints are each different and most scientists believe that every snowflake is also different.

Each snowflake is made up of thousands of tiny, identically shaped hexagonal crystals gathered together. And there are an infinite variety of snowflakes.

Wilson (Snowflake) Bentley, an American farmer who devoted most of his life to the examination and photography of snowflakes, never found two identical snowflakes.

And when comparing people, even twins have distinct differences.

Snow crystal forms generally fall into broad categories, or snowflake and ice crystal classifications, that are used to create a common form of reference to describe snow crystals.

So let's "dig in" and see what lessons we can learn from snowflakes.

In the Bible, Job is admonished to "Stop and consider the wondrous works of God."

And you, dear reader, are indeed a wondrous work of God!

THINK ABOUT

I Thessalonians 5:11 "Therefore encourage one another and build one another up, just as you are doing."

Philippians 4:8 "Finally, brothers, whatever is true, whatever is honorable, whatever is just, whatever is pure, whatever is lovely, whatever is commendable, if there is any excellence, if there is anything worthy of praise, think about these things."

1. Try using the graphic organizer to compare snowflakes and people.

2. Help your child or grandchildren make their fingerprints on a piece of paper.

3. Teachers: Invite a fingerprint expert to visit your room and give a presentation.

4. During the first snowfall of the season, head outside with magnifying glasses and a piece of dark construction paper to examine firsthand the loveliness of the snowflakes.

CHAPTER TWO

"The Snowflake Speech"

All over the world young people enter the classrooms each Fall. They are excited about seeing old friends and anticipate meeting their new teacher.

Our classroom teachers are excited to meet their new students and make a difference in their lives.

Along with their regular subjects, students may become part of the music program, a school sport's team, debate club, student government, or the art fair. Some children love to work in a group and others work best individually.

It is important for the new teachers to get to know their students well.

Some students' talents are easy to spot or measure with standardized tests.

Others can only be seen by careful observation.

Parents please remember this when looking over your child's report card. Your child may struggle with reading or math but don't overlook something amazing that your child might be able to do in another area.

As a teacher it is crucial to make note of these observations. We must not let students with unusual or less observable skills get overlooked in the race to post the highest reading and math scores in the district.

If we truly believe that God has made each human being with different skills and talents, how can we logically expect the following year's scores to get better and better? Instead, each year's scores should fluctuate, reflecting the individuality of students in that year's classroom.

Or how could we logically compare teacher A to teacher B when those two teachers have distinctly different individuals in their classrooms. And every year there will be different intelligences in those classrooms.

Yes, educators need to always strive for excellence and mastery of important skills, but we also need to develop a philosophy in education of developing the strengths of the individual. Otherwise our schools will become factories.

Factories turn out lots of exactly the same thing, over and over.

If we truly believe that each individual is unique, then this is not what we really want for our children.

Seasoned teachers have little things that they look for in their students. The power of observation is an amazing tool that helps the instructor begin to get a picture of what the future may hold for each child.

Many of the most important observations will be made outside the structured classroom setting.

Perhaps the talent or skill will become obvious at lunch, on the playground, or during a fieldtrip.

The great teacher or significant adult role model will always be looking for what makes that child unusual.

Before the first snowfall of the season our classes had many opportunities to play a variety of games with their classmates. Usually everyone enjoyed playing these games with their friends. It was a great way to teach, to review, to aid in memorization, and to practice people skills.

Every one of my classes was made up of very different individuals. Those cute, little first graders all came to the classroom with various life experiences and divergent attitudes towards learning.

I also believe that God blessed every student with distinct intelligences as well.

However, there are some things we all loved to do as students. Maybe you remember your favorite educational game in school.

Individual and team games motivate students to practice the things they have learned and make learning fun.

`We played the fly swatter game, phonics games, Shake Those Beans, Sparkle, and even the old standard, Around the World.

But inevitably, when the winner was finally determined, there were a few tears and even some anger from the losers.

Occasionally there were some way too proud winners!

By this time in the year we were seeing the first snowflakes falling outside our window.

On that day we would stop what we were doing and take several minutes to silently gaze at the beauty of the snowflakes falling outside our classroom. Then I would call everyone to sit on the floor together near my chair and give the annual "Snowflake Speech":

"Everyone in this room is uniquely created by God with special talents and skills.

Your parents and your teacher and even other students in this room are going to begin to notice those gifts.

You will not all be good at the same things. And that's okay!

Some of you will be wonderful readers and spellers.

Some of you will be amazing writers that will make us cry, or laugh, or stop to think long and hard about what you have said.

Some of you will excel in math and beat everyone on the timed tests and games.

Some of you will be outstanding in sports, draw beautiful pictures, or touch our hearts with your music.

Some of you will be great leaders. You will encourage your friends to be their very best. You will lead them to do great and mighty things.

Some of you will be deep thinkers and solve all kinds of problems all by yourself. You will make us think more deeply because of your amazing ideas and thought-provoking questions.

Some of you will be able to fix things that are broken in our room or at home. You may even find a new way to do something.

Some of you will help settle problems between your friends. (Blessed are the peacemakers.)

Some of you will cheer us all up by saying or doing something extremely funny just when we need it the most.

When one of your friends in this class does one of these things this year, be proud of them and let them know how well they did.

When someone tells you that you did well, remember that this may be one of the talents or skills that God has given you. Learn to use it for His glory while you are here on this earth.

Don't cry or get mad when you lose.

Don't get discouraged and give up trying.

Determine to always do your best. Praise others when they do well and enjoy finding out about your own special gifts.

Don't brag about your accomplishments to others.

The Bible tells us in Proverbs 27:2 to "Let another praise you, and not your own mouth."

Use the power of observation to discover what talents God has given you and your friends.

Don't expect to be like your sister, or your brother, or a cousin, or your father or mother.

You are unique! It is what makes the world such a wonderful and exciting place to live.

How boring and predictable it would be if everyone were exactly the same.

You are unique . . . a beautiful masterpiece of God, just like those lovely snowflakes you see falling outside our window!"

At this point, I must add the following comment for parents.

Parents please do not ever tell your child that you wish they were more like their sister or brother.

We can never be like our siblings because, just like snowflakes, there are no two of us exactly alike.

I cannot begin to tell you the damage that those words can do to a child.

I have seen it happen to some very dear people and in some cases it has kept them from reaching the potential that should have been theirs.

What you will learn in the next pages will help you to become more aware of the multiple intelligences and the different strengths and weaknesses that may characterize certain birth orders.

The world is probably very glad that people like Abraham Lincoln, Laura Ingalls Wilder, Babe Ruth, Albert Einstein, Susan B. Anthony, Martin Luther King, Jr., Amelia Earhart, Jackie Robinson, Marian Anderson, and Billy Graham were not like their brother or sister.

Just like snowflakes, they made a beautiful impact on their landscape.

THINK ABOUT

Ephesian 2:10 "For we are God's masterpiece. He has created us anew in Christ Jesus, so we can do the good things he planned for us long ago."

Romans 12:6-8 "We have different gifts, according to the grace given us. If a man's gift is prophesying let him use it in proportion to his faith. If it is serving, let him serve; if it is teaching, let him teach; if it is encouraging, let him encourage; if it is contributing to the needs of others, let him give generously; if it is leadership, let him govern diligently; if it is showing mercy, let him do it cheerfully."

1. Make a list of things that you think you are good at doing or enjoy doing.

2. What was your favorite subject in school?

3. What do you enjoy doing in your free time?

CHAPTER THREE

"The First Snowfall of the Year"

Because of the different climates, some areas of our world never, or rarely, see a beautiful snowflake.

Our Texas granddaughter recently saw an unusual amount of snowflake activity outside of her home. I am sure it was an exciting day for her and all her little west Texas friends as they stared out the window at the beautiful display of God's handiwork.

She really looks at those snowflakes. She studies them carefully and admires each one.

In Ohio our other three grandchildren see many snowflakes every winter. Their parents probably become very weary of driving those snow-covered roads and shoveling their walks.

Sometimes snowflakes are hardly noticed at all. People are too busy trying to negotiate their way safely here and there and wondering when Spring will finally come.

For various reasons, young people, too, are often overlooked in this life.

Parents are busy working two jobs. There is little time at night to really notice what makes each one of their children talented or special. Important words of affirmation are not bestowed on those who might need it most.

As educators our ever-changing curriculums and programs, and large class sizes make it extremely difficult to look for talents and skills in individual students.

Good teachers try hard to spend quality time encouraging their students. They often go home overwhelmed with thoughts of how they could have better met the needs of each child on that particular day.

In one of the following chapters I will share a powerful story about a very special boy who made an unusual observation. He exhibited an intelligence that encouraged him in front of our whole class.

I almost overlooked what he was trying to share with the class that day. Something told me to take the time to give his work a second look and I am so glad I did.

I have told his story over and over and always get the same amazing responses from those who hear it.

One of a teacher's highest goals is to be observant and to share what we observe with our students and their parents.

Sharing information with the principal can be useful as well.

Our building principal would usually hand out a special treat, sticker, or a certificate. I always knew that I could send a student there for recognition and encouragement.

Sometimes even our Superintendent would honor students for their achievements by dropping by for a visit. He loved to see what the students were accomplishing and listen to their opinions and ideas.

Acknowledgement is important but it doesn't have to be a big deal. "Snowflakes" just need to know that someone is noticing their work or special way of thinking.

Some children quietly go about doing things for others with a servant's heart. Their talent is silent and quiet like a gentle snowfall on a dark winter's night.

They may see someone with a heavy package heading for a closed door and run quietly ahead to open it for them.

They are always looking for ways to serve others. It brings them great joy but it is not a flashy talent.

Usually it is only a person who loves serving others that will be looking for these kinds of opportunities to help. They might become a pastor, missionary, policeman or fireman.

Snowflakes drift in and out of our lives. Some are people that we meet at the post office or the grocery store. It might be the furnace repairman, our electrician, daycare providers, or automobile mechanic.

If you are observant you will notice unusual things about each one that sets them apart and makes them special.

Take time to tell them what you appreciate about them.

Take time to notice. This will help them fall into their special place.

As teachers and parents, our lives are full of necessary things to do. Sometimes our children's accomplishments or talents can be easily overlooked if we do not take the time to "stand at the window and watch the snowfall".

Just recently I heard about a woman who was asked by her Sunday school teacher to read the scripture passage aloud for the class.

The teacher did not know that this woman struggled with reading.

Had the teacher known this woman a little better, I am sure that he would never have placed her in this situation.

When she was younger she did not receive the help that she needed. She failed to graduate from high school.

I found out that she was doing a job now that really didn't suit her and she often struggled financially.

Determinedly the woman began to read from her open Bible and finally managed to read through the entire passage. Her friends were all relieved and very proud of her.

In my mind, however, I was thinking about her former teachers and parents.

Why could they not get her the help that she needed?

Did they not see how she struggled and wonder why?

If someone had taken the time to notice this woman in her younger days they might have discovered her amazing aptitude for history.

It made her eyes light up and her face shine when she was speaking of historical events.

When you really took the time to observe, you could listen to her sharing things she saw and heard about on the history channel.

It is that sparkle that you see in peoples' eyes that lets you know they are passionate about something. Don't miss it because it could give a hint about their special gift.

Who knows what this lady could have done with her life if only someone had been there "watching the snowfall"!

My grandfather was a quiet man, a farmer by trade.

I never realized until much later, how talented he was at creating unique and useful pieces of machinery in his little machine shed.

If something broke on the tractor or equipment that he and his sons used, they would just take it into the shed and let Grandpa fool around with it for a while.

But it was very hard to get to know Grandpa because he was such a quiet man.

My Grandmother and I always had such a great time shopping in town or working in the garden or just talking. She loved to visit and she had many friends.

But Grandpa would always be busy in his shed or in the fields and preferred to spend time by himself.

At the end of a long day you would find him sitting quietly in his big chair by the window.

I remember thinking that he was a little odd because he would never really talk much.

Occasionally you could hear him whispering the words: "Thank-you, Jesus."

Now, as I look back, I believe that he was sitting in that chair contemplating God's mercy and goodness to him and to his family.

He was being grateful to God and setting an amazing example to his family about an "attitude of gratitude".

I am looking forward to thanking him for that Godly example when I see him in heaven someday.

Hopefully, as you read further in this book, you will be able to detect talents and skills that God has placed within your life and in those around you.

Using this knowledge will encourage the people you meet.

It will help them to become all that God has created them to be.

Please take time as adults to notice . . . to watch the snowfall.

If we don't notice, then these amazing "Snowflakes" may never have a chance to fall into their place.

They will just slowly melt away on the sidewalk in the sun or be swept away by the harsh winter wind.

THINK ABOUT

Job 37:10-12
The breath of God produces ice, and the broad waters become frozen. He loads the clouds with moisture; he scatters his lightning through them. At his direction they swirl around over the face of the whole earth to do whatever he commands them.

Job 37:14
"Stop and consider God's wonders."

Hebrews 10:24
"And let us consider how we may spur one another on toward love and good deeds."

1. Think about an important person in your life. What skill or talent do you think God has given them?

2. What is the most amazing thing that you have ever heard someone say or do?

CHAPTER FOUR

"Studying the Snow"
Multiple Intelligences

At the age of 60 I completed a "bucket list" goal and received by masters degree in education. I have always felt that it is important to be a lifelong learner and really enjoyed my classes at the university I attended.

Thankfully my dear husband, who probably deep inside thought I was a little crazy, never once criticized me. He encouraged me in my endeavor.

One of the many wonderful and life changing things that I studied in graduate school was the research by Dr. Howard Gardner on Multiple Intelligences.

In 1983 psychologist Howard Gardner proposed a different way of looking at intelligence. Instead of a single intelligence, Gardner believed that there were several and that every human being was intelligent, to a degree, in each one. These intelligences include:

- Visual-Spatial
- Bodily-Kinesthetic
- Musical
- Interpersonal

- Intrapersonal
- Verbal-Linguistic
- Logical-Mathematical
- Natural
- Existential (Spiritual)

Numerous tests and checklists have been developed which help people discover their abilities based on Gardner's research.

Many educators are familiar with the practical applications that this theory proposes. They see the benefits for their students in their ability to gain confidence and purpose for the skills and talents they possess.

Think back about your high school days.

Do you remember who you thought was the most intelligent person in your class?

Can you remember their name or names and what made you think that they were smart?

Did you think of those who were good in English, or math, or science?

You might have thought about the class valedictorian or perhaps the people who scored highest on their ACT tests.

I bet you didn't think about the star athlete, the 1st chair trombone player, or the person who fixed the old projector so that the teacher could use it one more year.

I cannot tell you the number of "snowflakes" I have known who felt that they were not smart because they did not receive good grades in school.

These students are similar to the beautiful snowflakes that fall where no one seems to notice them.

They lay there silently in forgotten snowdrifts.

They did not get high scores on the snowflake math test, or perhaps they fell down on the poor spelling snowdrift.

Just like those lovely snowflakes, we all have many outstanding characteristics but some may not be as noticeable as others.

Learning more about each of the multiple Intelligences will help us see how we have all been wonderfully and fearfully made.

We have each been blessed with special strengths and skills that make us useful and valuable in this world.

As you read through the remaining chapters of this book, you will be presented with information regarding each intelligence and birth order.

The following is a list of what these intelligences look like and what jobs might be a perfect fit for each one:

Linguistic intelligence This intelligence involves sensitivity to spoken and written language, the ability to learn languages, and the capacity to use language to accomplish certain goals. It includes the ability to effectively use language to express oneself rhetorically or poetically; and language as a means to remember information. Writers, poets, lawyers and speakers are among those that may have high linguistic intelligence.

Logical-mathematical intelligence This intelligence concerns the capacity to analyze problems logically, carry out mathematical operations, and investigate issues scientifically. In Howard Gardner's words, "It entails the ability to detect patterns, reason deductively and think logically. This intelligence is most often associated with scientific and mathematical thinking."

Careers to consider could include auditor, accountant, mathematician, scientist, statistician, computer analyst, and technician.

Musical intelligence This intelligence involves skill in the performance, composition, and appreciation of musical patterns. It is about the ability to recognize and compose musical pitches, tones, and rhythms. Sometimes musical intelligence can be related in structure to linguistic intelligence.

Job opportunities could include: musician, piano tuner, music therapist, choral director, or an orchestra conductor.

Bodily-kinesthetic intelligence This intelligence involves the potential of using one's whole body or parts of the body to solve problems. It is the ability to use mental skills to coordinate bodily movements. Sometimes there seems to be some connection between mental and physical activity.

If this sounds like you, you might enjoy becoming a physical therapist, dancer, actor, mechanic, carpenter, forest ranger, jeweler, or a professional athlete.

Spatial intelligence This one involves the potential to recognize and use the patterns of wide areas of space and more confined areas.

Folks with this intelligence might think about becoming an engineer, surveyor, architect, urban planner, graphic artist, interior decorator, photographer, or a pilot.

Interpersonal intelligence is concerned with the capacity to understand the intentions, motivations and desires of other people. It allows people to work well with others. Teachers, salespeople, political and religious leaders and counselors need a well-developed interpersonal intelligence.

Intrapersonal intelligence involves the ability to understand oneself and to appreciate our own feelings, fears and motivations. People with strong intrapersonal intelligence know their own strengths. Then they can use this information to live in a productive manner.

If you score high in this intelligence you might do well as a psychologist, therapist, counselor, theologian, program planner, or entrepreneur.

Natural Intelligence involves recognition, appreciation, and understanding of the natural world around you.

People with this intelligence usually choose to be outdoors and are familiar with various types of plants and animals. They enjoy many outside activities and perhaps own a pet.

People with natural intelligence might consider a career as a botanist, astronomer, wildlife illustrator, meteorologist, chef, geologist, or landscape architect.

In his book *Frames of Mind*, Gardner identifies qualities that you may see in individual children that could indicate their special strengths.

The phrases in parenthesis will help us get a better picture of each of the intelligences.

- Linguistic intelligence (word smart)
- Logical/mathematical Intelligence (number/reasoning smart)
- Spatial intelligence (picture smart)
- Bodily-Kinesthetic intelligence (body smart)
- Musical intelligence (music smart)
- Interpersonal intelligence (people smart)
- Intrapersonal intelligence (self smart)
- Naturalist intelligence (nature smart)

Gardner has also considered, but not included in his list, the possibility of Existential and/or Spiritual intelligence.

The previous information may have made you think about people you knew during your school days or people at your church or place of employment.

Hopefully it will make you think about what you like to do now or what you are good at doing. Usually it is more than one thing.

The theory of multiple intelligences and the study of birth order are very interesting.

Many of the ideas regarding multiple intelligence and birth order seem to line up with scripture regarding God's wondrous works of creation.

God created us and He has a wonderful plan for our lives. The stories and examples in this book will give you a deeper understanding of what that plan might look like.

We are blessed with all nine intelligences but some are obviously stronger in our lives than others. So use what you learn to find direction for yourself and for others who may be feeling rather unimportant or useless.

All of us need to have our spirits lifted from time to time.

The following stories are presented to encourage you to develop your own intelligence and do something you never felt possible.

Snowflakes fall to the ground and pile up.

They get carried into the school building on someone's new winter coat or boots where they quickly and silently melt.

Too often they are never really noticed.

Snowflakes are beautiful, but it's hard to see their unique structure unless you study them carefully.

Wonderfully Made by Megan Eddy

THINK ABOUT

James 1:17
"Every good and perfect gift is from above, coming down from the Father of the heavenly lights, who does not change like shifting shadows."

1 Corinthians 12:7-11
"But the manifestation of the Spirit is given to every man to profit withal. For to one is given by the Spirit the word of wisdom; to another the word of knowledge by the same Spirit; To another faith by the same Spirit; to another the gifts of healing by the same Spirit; To another the working of miracles; to another prophecy; to another discerning of spirits; to another [divers] kinds of tongues; to another the interpretation of tongues: But all these worketh that one and the selfsame Spirit, dividing to every man severally as he will."

Job 37:14 ". . . stop and consider the wondrous works of God."

1. Which of the multiple intelligences do you think are your own strongest gifts?

2. Think of something that someone has told you that they admire about you. Write it down here and think of some ways you could use this gift to help others.

3. What things have you often thought about learning to do? Pick one and get busy!

CHAPTER FIVE

"The Snowflake Man"

Many years ago there was a little boy who was fascinated with snowflakes. His name was Wilson Bentley.

There is a book about Bentley's life written especially for children.

Each year, after that first snowfall, I would try to read this book to my class.

Snowflake Bentley, the Caldecott Award book written by Jacqueline Briggs Martin and illustrated by Mary Azarian, poetically reveals the life of the photographer and farmer, Wilson Bentley.

As a little boy he became fascinated with snowflakes.

Fortunately he grew up in an area of Vermont called the "Snowbelt," which received up to 120 inches of snowfall each year.

He loved to be outside studying the things he found there and often drew pictures of them.

These two facts alone would indicate that Bentley probably possessed natural intelligence and spatial intelligence and will be examined later in this book.

Educated at home, young Bentley spent many winter hours studying individual snowflakes. He identified their hexagonal shape and drew hundreds of pictures.

At age 17, Bentley's parents, seeing his interest, bought him a special camera that worked with a microscope. He began to photograph the snowflakes that he was so passionate about.

Throughout his life, Bentley refined his photography, capturing images of thousands of snowflakes, no two alike.

At age 66, a book of his work was published. This book brought the beauty and wonder of the Vermont snow to people all over the world.

Willie Bentley, (Snowflake Bentley) was fascinated with snowflakes. His photographs and information are widely used by the scientific world and anyone who takes the time to admire God's beautiful creation. He was a pioneer in the photography of very small objects (photomicrography), and he absolutely loved what he did.

> *"I wouldn't trade places with Henry Ford or John Rockefeller for all their millions! And I wouldn't change places with a king: not for all his power and glory. I have my snowflakes!"*
>
> *Wilson A. Bentley*

Bentley's parents, no doubt, were busy farmers. What if they had not taken the time to encourage their son in his desire to learn more about snowflakes?

What if they had not helped him with the purchase of special cameras to film what he saw?

Perhaps there were some who felt that spending so much effort studying snowflakes was a waste of time.

Today Wilson Bentley's photographs are the ultimate source of information regarding the science of snow crystals. Scientists all over the world refer to his work.

People of all ages enjoy the incredible pictures and the story of his boyhood hobby.

Read this book to a child or for your own pleasure. It will inspire and encourage everyone and the pictures are amazing!

That first snowfall is so beautiful and almost breathtaking, especially if you don't get to see snow very often.

Look at your own snowflakes carefully to examine their individual size and structure.

No wonder so many of my students, even in Iowa, would excitedly run to the window to see that first snowfall of the season.

Maybe you, too, enjoy watching those first, fluffy flakes fall from the sky.

All of us are somewhat like the snowflakes that Wilson Bentley intently studied. We are an amazing creation of God.

Use your power of observation as you read more about the different intelligences and birth order characteristics discussed in this book. You will be looking at each person in your life in a new way.

You may be seeing talents and skills that have surrounded you for many years.

With the information from this book you will find out how God can use these talents to make an eternal difference.

Try taking an online multiple intelligence test. There are several that you can fill out and quickly find where your own strengths lie.

The first snowfall is a time of wonder and awe.

Sometimes in the classroom I would have to finally draw the blinds or curtain so that we could all get back to work.

But I always took time for the students to see that first snowfall of the winter. It is a delightful sight!

Taking time is the key!

We are such a busy generation aren't we? (Curriculum to get through, new ideas to explore, tests to take, reports to write.)

And as parents you know what busy is!

You help your child with their homework, go to work, keep up with the laundry and housework, and complete numerous home repairs. There are cars that need work and trips to gymnastic practice, soccer practice, and away games.

And what about our church programs? In some churches there is something going on every night of the week it seems. And it is all great stuff!

Wilson Bentley's parents were also busy with the work of life, but because of their encouragement he found something that fascinated him.

He was able to develop his scientific abilities and discover all that he could about a subject that was dear to his heart.

With their help God's purpose for his life began falling into place.

> *"Under the microscope, I found that snowflakes were miracles of beauty; and it seemed a shame that this beauty should not be seen and appreciated by others. Every crystal was a masterpiece of design and no one design was ever repeated. When a snowflake melted, that design was forever lost. Just that much beauty was gone, without leaving any record behind.*
> Wilson "Snowflake" Bentley 1925

THINK ABOUT

Philippians 2:13 "For it is God who is at work in you, both to will and to work for His good pleasure."

Jeremiah 29:11 "For I know the plans that I have for you,' declares the LORD, plans for welfare and not for calamity to give you a future and a hope."

Proverbs 3:5-6 "Trust in the LORD with all your heart, and do not lean on your own understanding. In all your ways acknowledge Him, and He will make your paths straight."

1. If you are a parent or grandparent, make a list of the talents that you see in the lives of each of your children and/or grandchildren. Share your list with them.

2. Take time to do one of the multiple intelligence tests that are mentioned on the website at the end of this book or write down what you think are your 4 strongest intelligences.

CHAPTER SIX

"The Winter Wonderland of Words"
Verbal-Linguistic Intelligence

My students had been working on a writing project one beautiful Fall day.

Some had been working diligently to complete their assignment.

Some were struggling with the topic that had been given to them.

And some students had written a few words and skipped right on to the top part of the paper. The top part was entirely blank and left them room to draw a picture about their writing.

I gave them a few more minutes while the soothing, beautiful, classical music played softly in the back of the classroom.

It was a quiet, contemplative time in Room 150.

Sometimes we just need time to think about things, don't we?

I rang the little bell on my desk indicating a few minutes to quickly wrap up what they were writing. Then we all gathered in the back of the room with our writing journals.

The students sat on the big rug with their friends and neighbors and anticipated sharing what they had written.

For various reasons, not everyone would want to share their thoughts on this particular day.

Some had found the topic uninteresting.

Some simply had not been able to relate with the selected topic.

The artists in the room had spent way too much time drawing their picture or thinking about what transpired on the playground earlier in the day.

One or two of the students would leave us mesmerized with powerful words and thoughts that they had written in their journal.

I always told my students that great writing would make us feel some emotion such as laughter, sadness, or even anger.

Many of our students were talented writers but I will always remember one little girl with beautiful, dark hair and a captivating smile.

Whenever Linette would share her stories, the class would grow quiet with anticipation. They had listened to her stories before and were anticipating something great. She had a real talent for writing and never failed to impress us with her thoughts and creative abilities.

Sometimes her stories would make us laugh.

Sometimes they would leave us with tears in our eyes.

Once in awhile the room would grow completely silent after hearing one of her presentations because her words had touched our hearts so deeply. Great writing often does just that.

I saw this young lady at school one day recently. She was in 5th grade and one of her friends excitedly came up to me to tell me about her latest work.

Her fellow students and teachers are such an encouragement to her as she continues to develop her talent.

Perhaps one day we will see her writing in print. God has given her an amazing talent for drawing with words.

I hope that she will always be inspired by our admiration of her skills long ago when we began to notice them in first grade.

One day while checking out at the grocery store I struck up a conversation with a high school student who was "ringing me up".

As she was helping me get the groceries into my cart I asked her what her plans for the future were as she headed off to college.

I was immediately taken with the fact that she was fluent in four languages and anticipated a possible career in foreign diplomacy or the United Nations.

What an amazing gift!

Not everyone is talented in speaking a different language. Some of us just want to speak and write our own language a little better!

Twice a month I get a manicure at Artist Nails in my hometown of Altoona, Iowa. I am always impressed with the way the owners and their staff have been able to learn the English language. They easily flip back and forth between Vietnamese and English at such a rapid pace that it boggles my mind. Their clients have reaped the benefits from their perseverance at learning another language.

This local shop is known for its friendly, customer service and does a thriving business in our community. Customers notice and appreciate their efforts to communicate.

While in Bangkok, Thailand, my youngest son and I taught English to students at one of the public elementary schools as well as a special adult class in the evening.

The missionary family that we stayed with, Ricky and Tammy Salmons, have done such a fantastic job of learning the Thai language.

They also utilize sign language to work with the deaf people in their area of Bangkok. This special gift allows them to translate for businesses and government groups as well as working with a very talented, deaf, soccer team.

Many people have been encouraged and blessed because of the way these dear missionaries use their verbal-linguistic intelligence.

I admire the way people can learn a new language. To me it seems an impossible task requiring much perseverance. Some of you may feel the same way. It is just not our strongest intelligence and that is okay!

There are numerous examples of great American leaders, who were blessed with the power of words and made a great impact on history.

One of my favorite stories is about a man who left a rich legacy in our United States History.

This interesting account clearly relates how a person, who had a real way with words, was led to believe that he was a failure simply because of the lack of response from those around him.

History went on to record that the man did, indeed, have a marvelous and powerful way with words. Hopefully he was able to understand the effect of those words before his untimely death.

In the 1860's Americans fought one of the saddest wars in our history, the Civil War.

On a little piece of land in Gettysburg, Pennsylvania, many Union and Confederate soldiers died in a terrible and bloody battle.

On November 19, 1863, people gathered to dedicate a cemetery and honor the soldiers who were buried there.

Edward Everett, a famous speaker from Massachusetts, gave a long and eloquent speech honoring the fallen soldiers. He spoke for over an hour.

Even though it was a very long speech everyone loudly applauded the magnificent words they had just heard.

The last speech of the day was to be given by the President of the United States.

Abraham Lincoln Delivers the Gettysburg Address
by Rylan Harmeyer

President Lincoln had hastily written his speech on a scrap of paper while traveling to Pennsylvania by train.

Historians note that President Lincoln was not well at the time and even complained of feeling light-headed. However he had taken the long train ride from Washington to honor the men and nation that he cared about so deeply.

The words he wanted to share with the crowd that day were running over and over through his mind.

He arose to speak and just two short minutes later those quickly written notes had been completely shared with the audience.

It is reported that an odd silence came over the crowd. There was little, if any, clapping. Lincoln returned to his seat.

Eventually he boarded the train to return to Washington feeling that his speech and thoughts had been an utter failure. The hushed response from the audience surely made him feel foolish and ineffective. They had clapped long and hard for Mr. Everett. Why not for him?

Newspapers of the day that were not aligned with Lincoln's political party criticized his speech for its shortness and inappropriateness at such a solemn event.

But today, over 100 years later, the true report is known.

Lincoln's Gettysburg Address, presented in a little over two minutes, is known as perhaps the most powerful and famous speech in American history.

I believe that the reason there was little response from the audience that day was because they were stunned with the beauty and preciseness of the words that Lincoln used.

We can all relate to that feeling at one time or another in our lives when we have been witness to some amazing words of wisdom.

It might have been someone close to us, someone at our place of employment, or maybe a pastor or teacher.

Perhaps this verbal/linguistic intelligence is your special gift. Maybe someone has mentioned that you seem to have a "way with words".

If you know people who touch your heart and mind with the words they use, let them know.

President Lincoln returned to Washington, D.C. that afternoon feeling that he had failed miserably. However, the audience had just witnessed, first hand, the mighty power of verbal intelligence.

Hopefully Lincoln knew, before he died, what an impact his speech had made on our war-torn nation that chilly November day at Gettysburg.

"Four score and seven years ago . . ."

THINK ABOUT

Proverbs 16:24 "Gracious words are like a honeycomb, sweetness to the soul and health to the body."

Proverbs 25:11
"A word fitly spoken is like apples of gold in pictures of silver."

Ecclesiastes 9:17
"The words of wise men are heard in quiet more than the cry of him that ruleth among fools."

Ecclesiastes 10:12
"The words of a wise man's mouth are gracious . . ."

Daniel 1:4 ". . . youths in whom was no defect, who were good-looking, showing intelligence in every branch of wisdom, endowed with understanding and discerning knowledge, and who had ability for serving in the king's court; and he ordered him to teach them the literature and language of the Chaldeans."

1. What is your favorite quote or saying?

2. Who is your favorite author? Why?

3. Who is your favorite speaker? Why do you enjoy listening to them?

4. If one of your children or grandchildren enjoys writing, buy them a diary or journal notebook. Ask them to read their work to you from time to time.

CHAPTER SEVEN

"Deep Snow"
Logical/Mathematical Intelligence

Logical-Mathematical intelligence can be observed in many ways.

As you might have guessed, people with this intelligence usually excel in math. They are able to detect mathematical patterns and seem to have a real gift for reasoning. These folks quickly see the cause and effect of certain situations, love to ask questions, and are usually fond of working through problems to discover the answer.

Individuals with strong scores in this intelligence are also good at making inferences. They can quickly classify things by placing them in categories.

Deep thinkers enjoy wading through the snowdrifts of questions and problems that capture their attention.

They might be good at some of the following jobs: accountant, lawyer, auditor, banker, bookkeeper, computer analyst, scientist, and doctor.

Famous people with this intelligence might have been: Einstein, Galileo, Aristotle, Newton, Pythagoras, or Archimedes.

My dear husband seems to be blessed with this intelligence. He has the ability to look at things so logically. We often admire how he is able to present information in a way that makes perfect sense and is good at asking those important questions.

While discussing the day's events he will ask about certain things that leave me wondering, "Why didn't I ask that question?" or "Why didn't I find out about that?"

I am constantly amazed by his great communication with people.

Sometimes the logical/mathematical intelligence presented itself in my first grade classroom.

I will never forget the day I asked a little boy named Sam to tell the class how he had gotten his answer in math.

It was a simple first grade addition problem (9+2=11).

I expected him to tell the class about how he had added on from the highest number because that was what our lesson had been about for the past week.

But my mouth dropped open when he confidently began:

> "Well, Mrs. Wilson, I know that nine is an odd number and two is an even number. Whenever you add an even number to an odd number you always get an odd number. So I knew that the answer had to be 11 because 11 is the next odd number."

This was a six-year old child!

In nearly forty years of teaching I had never had a student explain the answer in this way!

You can imagine the silent looks of amazement that went around the room. Admiration for Sam's ability in math grew significantly on that particular day.

As soon as I could, I let the principal and superintendent know what we had just witnessed. (Keep an eye on the great potential in this child!) And of course I notified his parents.

"Deep Snow" thinkers like this young man have an ability to understand numbers and logical concepts more clearly than the rest of us.

They understand abstract analysis and function. Their reasoning skills are highly developed and they readily see numerical and logical patterns.

From that point on we knew that Sam had a special gift from God.

It may not seem like much to some of you, but teachers especially love to see an early glimpse of a child's intelligence.

It will give us all great joy in the future to hear what Sam and others like him are doing to serve the Lord who gave them their abilities.

The more you study math, even the fundamental things that were taught to 1st graders, the more you can see God's hand of creation in the patterns he gave to us.

These patterns often help us with the work we are called to do. People who have mathematical/logical intelligence are especially good at using these patterns to accomplish a variety of tasks. They see the patterns quickly.

Ways to Make 7		
Addend	Addend	Sum
0	7	7
1	6	7
2	5	7
3	4	7
4	3	7
5	2	7
6	1	7
7	0	7

7 Family Addition Pattern

For example, think about this simple pattern in addition. Notice in the table that as the numbers in the 1st column grow by one, the numbers in the middle column decrease by one. However the sum remains the same.

This pattern is true for all addition facts. Pointing out the pattern helps children when they first begin to add. It is just one of many patterns we see in math and in life.

God is the master mathematician and anyone who has studied the Bible cannot help but notice how many times the numbers 7, 10, 12, 40 and several other numbers are used.

There were the 7 days of creation, the 7th day a Sabbath, and the 7th year a sabbatical year.

In Revelations there are 7 churches mentioned. Jesus uttered 7 last sayings from the cross. Today there are 7 days in a week and 12 months in a year. There are 7 continents of the world.

Musicians will find it fascinating that there are seven white keys in an octave on the piano and if you add the black keys you get 12. There were 12 tribes of Israel and 12 disciples.

And consider the miracle of the loaves and fish. There 5 loaves and 2 fish and when everyone had eaten they collected 12 baskets of leftovers.

Today we have twelve months in a year, 12 inches in a foot, and a dozen eggs in a carton.

The Old Testament story of Joshua tells about the 7 priests marching around Jericho 7 times for 7 days with 7 trumpets.

It is easy to see that God has used certain numbers many times throughout the Bible, especially in creation but in many other areas as well.

In Iowa the snow could be heavy at times leaving behind great, fluffy drifts.

This deep snow was hard to wade through on the way home from school.

When we came to a sidewalk that had already been shoveled, it made that walk home a little easier to handle.

Seeing a path or "pattern" can also make learning much easier for those of us who do not score as high in logical-mathematical intelligence.

We appreciate you folks who are able to see the patterns and logically lead us to success.

When you share that path with the rest of us, we can all benefit.

Then we can get home quickly and spend the rest of the day making snow angels and building snowmen!

THINK ABOUT

Isaiah 1:18
"Come now, let us reason together . . ." says the Lord.

I Peter 3:15
"Now sanctify the Lord God in your hearts (minds); and always be prepared for (presenting) a logical defense to everyone who requests a reason from you concerning the hope which is among you, (doing so) with meekness and fear . . ."

I Thess. 5:21 "Prove all things; hold fast that which is good . . ."

Romans 12:2 "Do not conform any longer to the pattern of this world, but be transformed by the renewing of your mind. Then you will be able to test and approve what God's will is—his good, pleasing and perfect will."

1. Think about the patterns in your life. List a few and tell how they help you in your everyday life.

2. How do you think God uses patterns to help us?

3. Do you think that your life is a pattern for those around you?

4. If yes, what kind of a pattern are you displaying?

5. What kind of life pattern would you like to exhibit?

CHAPTER EIGHT

"Snowflake Song"
Musical Intelligence

It is the first chapel of the year at our school, Des Moines Christian.

All the classes from kindergarten through sixth grade begin marching into the multi-purpose room for some singing and a special guest speaker.

At this time of year, I am just beginning to know my students. Today I hope to find out a little bit more about their likes and dislikes and some of their special skills and talents.

The music begins and I turn my head to intently watch the students seated on the floor before me.

This is the time I always look forward to—the first chapel of the year! It is the day that I find out which of my students have musical intelligence.

Now if you love music you are already guessing how I can tell this about them.

The music begins and as I glance down the row of students I see some who are sitting quite still, not even their mouths are moving.

Some are singing along with the music teacher as she leads the students in praise and worship.

And a few are doing what musically intelligent people usually do. They move to the music, their heads, or their hands, or their whole bodies. And usually there is a smile on their face.

On this first day of chapel the music begins and a little boy, named Noah, begins to move to the music. His face lights up.

He was the only one in our class that day who really got "into" the music.

After chapel I approached him and asked, "Noah, you really liked that music in chapel today didn't you?"

"Oh yeah!" he replied. "Doesn't everyone?" (Only it really wasn't a question.)

I just smiled. I knew that one of these days he would realize that not everyone does like music as much as he does. And . . . that's okay.

I never did get to hear him sing but he had the rhythm thing down to an art! So did many others in the audience that day.

Music is very dear to my heart and it always amazed me that there were some students who could sit almost motionless through the entire song time.

There were students who did not excel in their regular classroom work. When it came to music however, it was the highlight of their day.

Some of our most famous musicians never really found their niche in the educational system. They were never recognized for their true ability until much later.

Singer Bruce Springsteen said of himself:

> "For me, I was somebody who was a smart young guy who didn't do very well in school. The basic system of education, I didn't fit in; my intelligence was elsewhere."

Singer, songwriter Ray Stevens wrote the song "Everything is Beautiful in It's Own Way".

While listening to the words one day I was struck with how well he sums up God's creation of mankind.

He starts his song with the familiar words of the children's chorus, "Jesus Loves the Little Children of the World" and then continues with:

> *Everything is beautiful in it's own way.*
> *Like the starry summer night,*
> *Or a snow-covered winter's day.*
> *And everybody's beautiful in their own way.*

Christian musicians like Michael W. Smith, Matt Redman, Chris Tomlin, and Laura Story have the snowflake song embedded in their hearts by a loving, heavenly father. God's gift of music flows out of them and into the lives of people all over the world.

Many of you reading this book are using the gift of music in your local church and various community groups. However, like other intelligences, we may be oblivious to the gift of music in our lives until an unusual event helps to bring it into focus.

When I was only six years old I was involved in a very traumatic accident while feeding my new puppy.

Father had sent me out to give the puppy some milk.

In those days the milk came in glass bottles.

When I walked onto the back step where his bowl was located, the puppy excitedly jumped up on me.

I fell down on top of the glass bottle, which broke on the cement sidewalk.

In an instant the broken glass cut deeply into my right arm and my screams of terror brought my father quickly to my aid.

Wrapping a towel around my arm, he grabbed me up and rushed me to the hospital emergency room a few blocks from our home.

Following a long recovery with some permanent damage to the tendons, and nerves, I began to slowly regain the use of my arm and fingers.

Eventually my Father got it into his mind that he needed to provide piano lessons for his daughter!

Dad was, no doubt, feeling a little guilty about what had happened to my arm on that terrifying day. So he found a dear, elderly lady who began to patiently teach me the fundamentals of playing the piano.

Never an amazing pianist, I did eventually learn to read music fairly well and then I began to sing along as I played.

It was something I really enjoyed and it provided great relaxation when I needed a break from schoolwork.

My family realized that I had a little talent in this area and soon I was taking voice lessons as well.

At the age of ten I sang a song and won a children's talent contest on one of our local, television stations.

Four years later I entered and won our church's National talent competition.

The prize for winning this competition was a scholarship to Cedarville College in Ohio.

Now this is really not the topic of this book but it is worth remembering that good things often come out of seemingly tragic accidents or events.

Those of you who play the piano or some other instrument know what a relaxing hobby this can be. You truly enjoy and appreciate God's gift of music in your life.

Musical intelligence displays itself in many ways.

My grandmother spent most of her life on a farm. She was active in her local church and she used her musical talent to bless the people who attended every Sunday.

This dear woman could play from the hymnbook for church services but her talent extended even further, to my great envy.

Grandmother could "play by ear"!

Sometimes I would ask her if she knew such and such a song.

She would reply, "I don't think I have heard that one before dear, but if you hum a few bars I can play it for you."

We can all probably think of people who are talented in that way.

And yet someone who cannot carry a tune, or who does not know how to play a musical instrument, can also have musical intelligence.

That dear husband of mine also loves to listen to music. He enjoys the latest praise and gospel music as well as the familiar hymns of our younger days.

As a truck driver he is on the road for long hours and has an opportunity to listen to music while driving along those Iowa interstates.

He knows the words to the songs and he knows the names of the artists and their groups.

The part that I really admire is that the words and music touch his life and mine as he plays his favorite songs for me.

We certainly do not have to sing or play a musical instrument to possess musical intelligence.

Just recently a friend of mine on Facebook posted a funny dog video that made me wonder if even animals are affected by music.

The owner of this beautiful golden retriever was playing their guitar which you could hear in the background of the video.

As long as the guitar was playing, the dog's head was gently swaying to the rhythm and it had a happy smile. Whenever the guitar stopped (on purpose, I suspect) the dog's head stopped moving and the smile disappeared. This happened over and over to make it clear to the viewer that the music was making the dog respond. It was quite funny!

Everywhere we go, we see people who are listening to the music. They can easily be spotted waiting in line at one of the local businesses.

Their bodies may be gently moving to the rhythm or their lips silently singing along to a song in their mind.

Some folks can get quite animated and make us chuckle to ourselves at their obvious enjoyment of music.

These music lovers may be way off tune but the gift of music is certainly making their day a lot brighter.

Many of you folks who love music are using that gift in your local church as a music leader, or as a music teacher, or a member of an orchestra.

Your job may be to plan wonderful concerts for us to attend that will lift our spirits just when we need it most.

At times educators use music to help students remember new concepts.

Did you ever learn something in school because your teacher taught it to you in the format of a song?

Several of us still hum the ABC song in order to think of something in alphabetical order.

Scripture verses and names of the books of the Bible are often taught to children as a song.

I can still sing a little Bible song that I learned as a child which helps me remember all the names of the sons of Jacob.

Our daughter has always enjoyed music. Now that she is older she loves to make up songs for preschool children that go along with a particular theme or lesson for the week.

People who are good at this kind of thing are also exhibiting strengths in verbal-linguistic intelligence.

Our youngest son enjoys putting just the right music together with videos that he makes. I am always in awe of the way he finds just the right song and adds it to each particular video.

God has used this musical talent in his life in many ways.

The background music he chooses for his video creations have made a special memory for a friend's wedding,

The cross-country team he helps to coach enjoyed seeing the highlights of their year together with a great song playing in the background.

His older brother, a pastor in Texas, was the benefactor of some wonderful video introductions for a series of messages he presented to his church.

And my Mother's Day video will always hold a very special place in my heart.

There are at least 1150 verses in the Bible that refer to some form of music such as Psalm 100:2. "Serve the Lord with gladness; Come before His presence with singing."

David in the Bible must have enjoyed playing on his little harp while he watched those wooly sheep. Perhaps it helped to make the long, lonely hours with the flock go by more quickly.

Later on in life David even used the gift of music to help comfort a troubled King Saul.

Certain kinds of music do have a way of relaxing and soothing our minds and bodies.

We can sometimes hear this kind of music playing quietly in the background at many of our favorite stores and businesses. It certainly plays an integral part in preparing the congregation for worship each Sunday.

Many people are blessed with musical intelligence. Think about the people you know who are talented in this area. Take time to thank them.

They entertain, educate, and encourage us with God's wonderful gift of music.

Singing Snowman by Hallie Creighton

THINK ABOUT

Exodus 15:2 "The Lord *is* my strength and song, And He has become my salvation; He *is* my God, and I will praise Him; My father's God, and I will exalt Him."

Psalm 69:30 "I will praise God's name in song and glorify him with thanksgiving."

Psalm 98:4 "Make a joyful noise unto the Lord, all the earth: make a loud noise, and rejoice, and sing praise."

1. What kind of music do you enjoy the most? Why do you think it is your favorite?

2. Who is your favorite singer? Why?

3. If you could play any instrument, what would you pick?

4. Do you enjoy the words or the music or both?

CHAPTER NINE

"Snow-Shovelers"
Bodily-Kinesthetic Intelligence

When we think of bodily-kinesthetic intelligence we usually think of athletes. Someone like Michael Jordan, Babe Ruth, Jesse Owens, or gymnast Shawn Johnson might come to your mind.

Many of us admire people who have athletic ability and perhaps wish that God had given us more strength in this area. At times I often wonder if there is even a tiny drop of this intelligence in my entire genetic structure!

Some of us can trip just walking down the sidewalk and do serious damage to various body parts in two seconds flat. Perhaps you have wondered if you were just a natural born klutz!

However, when participating in some kind of physical activity those of you with verbal intelligence may come up with some of your best ideas.

There is something about moving that helps us focus our thoughts and put them into words.

Sometimes just getting up and taking a walk often helps me think of some creative ideas or just the right words or picture to use when preparing a special presentation or document.

If you are trying to focus on how to address a particularly troublesome situation, it might help to stand and stretch or move around a bit.

German philosopher Friedrich Nietzsche is quoted as saying, "All truly great thoughts are conceived while walking."

Many times my best ideas have come during those moments when I have dragged myself outside and put one foot in front of the other for 40 minutes.

As I meander along the familiar streets of my hometown here in Iowa I have time to contemplate God's blessings and His purpose for my life.

He has given me some great ideas that help me compare Biblical truths with the things I see along my walk.

So even klutzy people, who do not really enjoy physical activity, can get ideas and accomplish their goals when they move around a bit.

There is actually some very interesting research that has been done on the effect of chewing gum before taking a test. Just the simple act of moving their jaws helped the students in these studies stay more alert and do a better job on their tests.

Bodily-kinesthetic intelligence is characterized by strength in physical movement and fine motor control.

Good eye-hand coordination and dexterity are characteristics of those who are blessed with this intelligence.

They tend to remember things by doing them rather than seeing or hearing about them.

People with strong bodily-kinesthetic intelligence might become actors, or artists, or builders, or of course, athletes.

They are our "Snow-Shovelers" and they are out there moving.

These bodily-kinesthetic people need to experience first-hand by actually doing the work, or process, or steps.

If you show them a picture or tell them about it, they will learn.

However, they will really excel by using their bodies to complete the steps of the activity. It helps students understand a new concept and retain what they have just learned.

In order to teach a certain phonics rule in class I would make up an energetic, musical rap.

We would all stand and move our bodies to the rap as we chanted the new phonics rule. Like this favorite rap:

"L, S, and F often walk together at the end of a short vowel word."

The students seemed to love seeing their 64-year-old teacher doing such a silly thing with them.

Many of those students will remember that phonics rule as long as they live and spell those words correctly just because we moved our bodies while reciting the rule.

Our jobs often require us to become familiar with updated software or new software programs. These have been implemented in our schools to promote better communication with busy parents and to help teachers with their student evaluations.

Programs such as these helped parents quickly access their children's grades online.

The software averaged and recorded the grades for quarterly reports and saved teachers a lot of time and effort.

But as any new process or skill, the first time you use it, it can seem over-whelming.

Some of you may have experienced the same thing at your place of employment recently.

After a few weeks you usually have a good handle on how to navigate the new programs or responsibilities.

We would always sit through a lot of presentations and be given information to read regarding the use of the new software. And although we all listened and watched intently to the presentations, it seemed very complicated.

We usually learned best by just getting onto our computers and trying it out.

You can see pictures and listen for directions on how to crochet, bake a cake, fix a flat tire, or change the oil in your car.

However, most of the people I know, who are really good at these things, have learned by doing.

Gardner's intelligences often overlap and that is because we are all talented in more than one area. We are just full of snowflake sparkle!

As you begin to see these intelligences in the people around you, remind them or tell them about that sparkle you see in their lives.

Sadly, many folks grow to adulthood thinking and feeling that they are not very intelligent.

We all need to know that God has given us amazing strengths and talents. We are all smart. We are just smart in different ways.

On the coldest day of the year in 2010 our furnace went out. And to make it even worse there was a blizzard raging outside.

I had called every repair service in town.

Either they did not answer or could not make it out to our home because of the roads or other calls.

We bundled up with blankets, turned on our electric heater, and managed to stay warm enough throughout the night.

First thing the next morning, our local repairman was able to get to our house and survey the situation.

We took him downstairs to the furnace room as my husband and I both wondered about how much a new furnace was probably going to cost us.

Our repairman took out his flashlight and began his examination.

Then, amazingly, he took out a small bottle of machine oil and sprayed a little on the fan.

The furnace fan started right up and within minutes heat started pouring out of the registers and warming up our icy, cold home.

As repairman Mike started putting away his tools and preparing to leave, I took the time to ask him how he learned to do what he did.

He told me that it all started when he was a little boy.

His mother had an old broken toaster sitting on the counter and he asked her if he could have it.

Since it was broken, his Mom gave him permission, knowing that it would probably keep his inquisitive mind occupied for hours.

You can imagine her surprise when, some time later, her little son brought the toaster back into the kitchen, plugged it in, and made himself some nice, warm toast.

There is an old phrase: "We learn by doing".

People with bodily-kinesthetic intelligence truly do learn by doing and they do it well. They often inspire all of us to strive for great things.

Major league pitcher, Jim Abbott, was born without a right hand. Despite this birth defect he pitched for the gold medal Olympic team in 1988 and threw a 4-0 no-hitter for the New York Yankees in 1993.

He loves to inspire others by telling them, "Find something you love, and go after it, with all of your heart."

Coaches make their athletes practice for hours on the court or field. Later on, at the big game of the week, we all enjoy watching them play.

You may have one of these athletic types in your family. They can often be a big help to us and certainly bring great enjoyment and energy into our lives.

Their gift to us is a little like that long walk home from school on a cold winter's day.

Those sidewalk "shovelers" were out there moving that snow. Because they had shoveled their sidewalks, it made the long walk home from school a little easier and much more enjoyable.

Thank-you, Lord, for the "snow-shovelers".

Shoveling Snow by Cece Sturdivant

THINK ABOUT

I Corinthians 9:24 "Know ye not that they which run in a race run all, but one receiveth the prize? So run, that ye may obtain."

Job 17:9 "The righteous keep moving forward, and those with clean hands become stronger and stronger."

Philippians 4:13 "I can do all things through Christ which strengtheneth me."

Hebrews 12:1 "Therefore, since we are surrounded by so great a cloud of witnesses, let us also lay aside every weight, and sin which clings so closely, and let us run with endurance the race that is set before us, looking to Jesus, the founder and perfecter of our faith, who for the joy that was set before him endured the cross, despising the shame, and is seated at the right hand of the throne of God."

Proverbs 24:5 "A wise man is strong; yea, a man of knowledge increaseth strength."

I Kings 3:14 "And if thou wilt walk in my ways, to keep my statutes and my commandments, as thy father David did walk, then I will lengthen thy days."

1. Try to spend more time exercising or walking this year. Keep a diary or journal of the ideas or solutions that come to you while you are doing these activities.

2. Make a list of people who have inspired the world with their special athletic ability. Find books about their lives and read them to your children or grandchildren.

3. Find someone in your community who is physically disabled and volunteer to help with a special project.

CHAPTER TEN

"Spatial Snowflakes"
Spatial Intelligence

People who have spatial intelligence usually think in pictures and use these mind pictures to remember information.

Snowflake pictures taken by Wilson Bentley, the "Snowflake Man" from Vermont, showed an amazing variety of breathtaking snowflakes. Bentley noticed that they were all very different except for one thing. Those beautiful snowflakes all had some form of hexagonal shape.

During your school days you might remember having learned that a hexagon has six sides.

Bentley's greatest joy was to take pictures of those sparkling flakes.

Before he was able to purchase his first camera he drew pictures of what he saw on paper.

He loved to study the structure of each individual snowflake.

Our youngest grandson often exhibits the gift of spatial intelligence, as well. He carefully observes how the things around him work and he learns by doing (bodily-kinesthetic).

One night while we were visiting him in Texas, the television show "Win It In a Minute" came on.

One of the crazy things that they asked a contestant to accomplish was stacking three golf balls in under a minute.

Now most of us, sitting there watching the show that night, were thinking how impossible that seemed and indeed the contestant failed to get the job done in that short amount of time.

However, this little five-year old went straight out to the garage to his father's golf bag and returned a few minutes later with three golf balls in hand.

We adults continued visiting as this determined little guy sat up shop on the smooth kitchen counter and proceeded to practice stacking those golf balls.

Occasionally I would glance his way and could see him carefully studying the surface of each ball.

And yes, he did stack three golf balls in under a minute, over, and over, and over. I have picture of it!

The more we watched him do it we learned what he discovered from his observations and practice.

Each golf ball has little dimples on its surface and those little dimples are what allowed him to stack the balls one on top of another.

One of this little boy's distant relatives was Nikola Tesla, the inventor of alternating current electricity and the radio.

Most scientific work is done by trial and error but Tesla was able to visualize his work before it even became a reality.

His amazing intelligence allowed him to recite entire books from memory. He was able to design machines in his head rather than drawing them out on paper.

Tesla saw the pictures in his mind and could recall them at any time.

People often made fun of him for proposing impossible inventions and then he went ahead and invented them anyway.

This unusual ability is sometimes called synesthesia. I mention it in this book for an important reason. I often wonder if this man would have illuminated the world with even more fantastic inventions if only someone had understood his great intelligence instead of making fun of it.

Unlike some of the other famous inventors of the day, Tesla's greatest desire was to help others. Making money and acquiring fame were not important to him although it did bother him when others took credit for his work or made fun of his ideas.

Although not well known, Nikola Tesla's inventions have perhaps made the most significant impact on the world in the last two centuries.

One of you may have a very special intelligence or live or work with someone who exhibits unusual skills.

We all need to do a better job noticing and validating what we see in the lives of the people around us. God has given all of us some very special gifts.

As a young driver I often needed directions to get places and my Father would draw me a little picture.

When I could see the map it was easier for me to arrive at my destination.

Dad was an excellent artist. Whenever I needed something drawn by hand I would ask him for help. He could draw anything and we all knew it.

However some people do not realize that they have this spatial intelligence until much later in life. They may spend years doing a job that is not suited to them and not very fulfilling. When they were younger no one took the time to notice their special intelligence or encourage them in their endeavors. As a result, they missed the special place that God had for them to serve.

For some reason my mother decided, at the age of 40, to begin taking painting lessons.

None of us realized the extent of her talent until she brought home some of her work. We were totally amazed as she pulled out several landscape paintings and portraits. They were absolutely beautiful!

I asked her once why she had suddenly taken up painting and I will never forget her answer. She told me that she wanted to leave something for people to remember.

Two years later, at the age of 47, she was killed in a car accident just north of our hometown of Altoona.

Many of mother's things are now gone but her paintings remain.

We do, indeed, think of her often, especially when we see her lovely pictures hanging on the wall.

Snowflakes sometimes land in one place on the ground and then the wind blows them to a new place. They are still beautiful and treasured wherever they land.

"Spatial snowflakes" often enjoy looking at pictures, charts, movies, and maps.

Their interests might include: finishing puzzles, reading, writing, sketching, painting, or photography.

They often have a great sense of direction, too.

Career choices for these individuals might include: navigators, sculptors, artists, inventors, engineers, mechanics, architects, or interior designers.

There was a wonderful little boy whose story I often tell when I am doing presentations.

The story never fails to make an impression on those who hear it. It is an amazing example of why it is important to know about the differences in "snowflakes" (the multiple intelligences). You will know what makes that snowflake different from all the others and be able to comment on its beauty.

"Snowflakes" like to be noticed. It encourages them to "Sparkle"!

On this particular afternoon I was giving a math lesson and we were all sitting in the back of the room in a circle on the floor.

In the middle of the carpet I had placed a box of colorful, wooden, geo-shapes. There were little green triangles, red trapezoids, blue diamond shapes, some orange squares, and one yellow hexagon.

The assignment that day was to make a hexagon out of different shapes. The students had to tell us what shapes they needed and how many.

The first student started out by asking for six green triangles and quickly moved them together to make a perfect hexagon. It was just like the yellow one laying on the floor for an example. We all applauded.

The next child asked for two red trapezoids and then made another hexagon. Again there was clapping.

At the end of the lesson I began to give directions to line up for music class but I saw Emmett's hand go up. He excitedly informed us that he had one more way to make a hexagon.

As I looked at the clock I knew that the time was short before we needed to head out the door for music.

"Well, buddy, I think we've already found all the ways to make a hexagon. Are you sure you know a different way?"

He shook his head "Yes" confidently.

"So what do you need to make another hexagon for us today," I asked him politely but doubtfully.

"I need six squares."

My heart sank, knowing that there was not any way to make a hexagon with squares.

I began to give directions to the class for lining up and quickly forgot about Emmett working happily on the floor.

It wasn't long before he was done.

Just briefly I glanced down on the floor and gave him a quick thank you for trying his best.

But then, something made me stop and take a longer look.

I asked the children to all come back and sit down.

There on the floor, inside of six orange squares, was a perfect hexagon!

Hexagon Inside of 6 squares—Emmett Schelhaas

We had almost missed it.

We weren't thinking "outside the box".

"Do you see the hexagon?" I asked the class.

Some students saw it right away and excitedly shouted their approval.

Some had to have us point it out to them inside the six squares.

You can imagine how Emmett must have felt that day and how the students looked at him with new admiration.

Emmett's parents received a note after school detailing his amazing accomplishment.

On that lovely winter day the hexagons were literally appearing outside and inside our room and so we celebrated.

Snowflake celebrations are such fun!

We were late for music!

THINK ABOUT

Proverbs 2:10-11
"For wisdom will come into your heart, and knowledge will be pleasant to your soul; discretion will watch over you, understanding will guard you . . ."

Psalm 139:14
"I will praise Him for I am fearfully and wonderfully made."

Exodus 35:35
"Them hath he filled with wisdom of heart, to work all manner of work, of the engraver, and of the cunning workman, and of the embroiderer, in blue, and in purple, in scarlet, and in fine linen, and of the weaver, [even] of them that do any work, and of those that devise cunning work."

Isaiah 64:8
"But now, O LORD, thou [art] our father; we [are] the clay, and thou our potter; and we all [are] the work of thy hand."

1. What is your favorite art activity, craft, or hobby?

2. Are you or someone in your family talented in art? How do you use this gift to help or encourage others?

3. Try taking lessons or learning more about one of the activities in this chapter to see if you might have some talent in this area?

4. What is an art activity that you enjoyed in high school?

5. Learn to use a computer software program and create something you never dreamed you could do.

CHAPTER ELEVEN

"Social Snowflakes"
Interpersonal Intelligence

Snowmen are so interesting and occasionally in our hometown of Altoona, Iowa, I have seen some truly awesome and hilarious creations.

Sometimes you see them standing in a yard surrounded by happy, laughing children or you may see them standing all by themselves lost in thought.

People are like that, too.

There are some of us who only feel good when surrounded by friends and some of us who really enjoy being all by ourselves.

This chapter is about people with interpersonal intelligence.

If you have this intelligence you look forward to spending time with people.

These social snowflakes just love to be with other snowflakes.

They get so close and have so much fun that, before you know it, they become a snowball.

When they get together they "have a ball"!

They are just a "ball of fun"!

And eventually they are all enjoying each other's company so much that they make three balls and become a SNOWMAN!!!

I am sure that you get the idea by now that interpersonal people love being together to chat or do things together. They are people-people!

A little later on we will talk about birth order as well. It is interesting that many last-born children also have interpersonal intelligence.

They love being the life of the party. They love making people laugh and they learn at an early age that it is the easiest way to grab the attention away from those older siblings.

Interpersonal people want to be where the action is. Being around other people is important to them and they function well there.

People with interpersonal intelligence prefer the company of others.

These social snowflakes are good at understanding and interacting with other people.

They find it easy to understand the emotions of those around them and their intentions, and desires.

They usually know what motivates their friends and co-workers.

Interpersonal people are good verbal communicators but may also communicate quite well using non-verbal communication.

They can see things from different viewpoints and know how to develop good relationships with other people.

Folks with this intelligence usually have a very positive attitude and are good at resolving conflicts.

If this sounds like you or someone you know, then you might want to consider the following career choices:

- Psychologist
- Philosopher
- Counselor
- Sales person
- Politician

In education, many projects in the school setting require small groups to work together to solve a problem or prepare a presentation for the rest of the class.

Students would always exhibit many different levels of interpersonal intelligence.

Some students could hardly wait to get together and work. Most students would enjoy this kind of activity and working together was a good way to practice our people skills.

However there was usually at least one in every class who firmly preferred to work by themselves and finish the assigned task.

In the next chapter we will discuss how this intelligence differs from interpersonal intelligence.

Interpersonal people have "People Smarts". They are social and they love it.

If you ask how many friends they have, they will take the next twenty-five minutes and give you an exhaustive list of friends at church, work, the gym, the club, and the community. Other people usually enjoy being around them, too.

While out walking this past summer I happened to notice that some people in our small town spent a lot of time outside visiting with their neighbors in the evenings.

Almost without exception it was the same houses and families.

Even on the hottest nights of the summer these people were outside sitting in lawn chairs while their children played happily in and around the yard.

You could hear their talking and laughter from the street and they were obviously enjoying their time together.

On the 4th of July, Labor Day, and many weekends they had barbecues and parties in their yards.

We all have friends at school and church and within our community who love to host all kinds of parties in their homes.

They volunteer to host the storage container, cookware, jewelry, and beauty product parties.

They join clubs or start clubs and can't wait for the next big club meeting. Maybe these are the people who joined sororities and fraternities when they were in college. They usually prefer being where the action is.

If you work for a great company you can probably name people right now that you can count on as terrific, team players.

These people love to come alongside of others and work together to accomplish the task. They are such fun to work with and make those long days of overtime bearable.

In whatever group you are involved in, it is pretty easy to tell who your people-smart friends are.

All of us are blessed with each of the 9 intelligences. If we were to make a graph showing our strengths in each of those nine we would see some higher areas than others.

People-smart individuals are a good example of this.

At my water aerobics class there are many of us who are now retired. While visiting our class at the pool on any particular day you would notice a few of the ladies gathered in a small group and enjoying a friendly chat while working out. These would probably be your interpersonal ladies.

One or two of us will exercise the whole period without talking to anyone. These would be your intrapersonal folks that we will discuss in the next chapter.

And then there would be a few members who visit a bit but mostly exercise. They would be somewhere in between.

Educators are able to recognize students who have interpersonal intelligence just by observing student behavior on the playground or in the classroom.

Children with this intelligence tend to spend their time playing tag, basketball, or other large group games where they can interact with lots of people.

They really enjoy working on group activities in the classroom and rarely argue about how to accomplish the task. They know that they just want to work on it together.

Many of our dear pastors and teachers are blessed with strong interpersonal intelligence. They are able to make a significant impact on the people they shepherd and teach.

"People-People" are concerned about the needs of others and seek them out to ask about their welfare or help them attain their goals.

Usually their voice messaging systems are jam-packed with calls. Communication is a very important part of the ministry in which God has placed them.

These social snowflakes are blessed with an outstanding gift from God.

Many jobs would never be completed if it weren't for the team players and the wonderful way that they get together and "get-er-done".

And, of course, it would be hard to make a snowman without them!

Children Playing in the Snow by Carter Sanders

THINK ABOUT

Romans 15:5-6
"May the God of endurance and encouragement grant you to live in such harmony with one another, in accord with Christ Jesus, that together you may with one voice glorify the God and Father of our Lord Jesus Christ."

Proverbs 27:17
"As iron sharpens iron, so one man sharpens another."

Ecclesiastes 4:9,10 "Two are better than one, because they have a good return for their work; If one falls down, his friend can help him up. But pity the man who falls and has no one to help him up!"

Hebrews 10:24,25 "And let us consider how to stir up one another to love and good works, not neglecting to meet together, as is the habit of some, but encouraging one another, and all the more as you see the Day drawing near."

1. Given the choice would you prefer to spend your time with your friends or by yourself?

2. What kinds of activities do you enjoy when you are with your friends?

3. Which of your children or grandchildren seem to exhibit strengths in interpersonal intelligence? Help them choose the best group activities for their age and interest levels.

CHAPTER TWELVE

"Silent, Sensitive Snowflakes"
Intrapersonal Intelligence

People who have intrapersonal intelligence know a lot about themselves and their own inner feelings. They know what they fear, the problems they struggle with, and their hopes for the future.

This intelligence is often summarized as "Self Smart" and these folks really enjoy having time to be all by themselves.

Intrapersonal people know their own strengths and weaknesses. They like to think about things and tend to analyze themselves, sometimes over analyzing.

There are many different jobs in which strong intrapersonal people excel. These jobs include: artists, researchers, philosophers, actors, psychologists, inventors, and writers.

Intrapersonal people work well with personal goals and deadlines. They often prefer to work by themselves instead of in a group in order to get work done.

One snowy day all three classes of our 1st grade students were working in a large room called the Multi-Purpose Room (MPR).

The assignment was to make large posters about a lesson we had just had in science.

Most of the students were excited about getting out of their rooms and doing a special project in small groups with their friends.

Drawing was involved as well as writing a short sentence or two. Every group could pretty much decide what they wanted to do and how they wanted to do it within the framework of the lesson.

One little girl's group was really struggling to even get started.

After observing her group for several minutes, I realized that the problem might be that this little girl had intrapersonal intelligence. She really preferred to work by herself and just get the job done! She was struggling with efforts by her friends to decide who would be responsible for each part of the project.

Quietly I asked this little girl if she would like to have a seat over at a separate table. I would make sure that she had her own paper and crayons to complete the project.

I knew I was right when the sparkle came back into her face and eyes. She was silently thanking me for the opportunity to work alone and needed time to think about how to get the job done.

She couldn't do that with all those people around her and within minutes she had made her plan. The other girls made their plan, and the projects were completed.

Having intrapersonal intelligence does not mean that you are rude, unfriendly, or a hermit.

There are times when intrapersonal people love being with others, too. However if you asked them to choose, they would usually prefer to have some quality time by themselves.

In areas where children see a lot of snow, the teachers are often forced to keep the students inside for recess.

When temperatures drop below 10 degrees it is just too cold to send those little people outside.

On those very cold days, teachers usually have a cupboard of "inside recess" games or at least a list of approved activities for students to enjoy while having a break in their room.

It is easy to spot the students who might score high in intrapersonal intelligence during these inside recess periods. They can be found sitting by themselves having a great time quietly reading a good book. You might also find them playing a game on the class IPod or computer, or just drawing a picture all by themselves in a corner of the room.

They usually have one or two dear friends that they enjoy spending time with but they are quite content with their own company.

Perhaps you feel the same way. You just need your "Me" time. And that is okay.

Sometimes you will want to connect with others. Be sure to try getting involved by joining a local exercise group, volunteering at your child's elementary school, or at the town library. You could participate in Bible study groups at your church or in the community. These are all good ways to interact with others and God certainly needs us all to minister to one another.

Silent-sensitive snowflakes do need their quiet time however. We all do at one time or another.

Being able to think about the day's activities and many other things that are going on in our lives is important.

Of course, that is when God speaks to us as well. We are setting some time aside to read his word and to really think about what He is teaching us.

Not everyone was created by God to be a social snowflake.

Some of us are the kind of snowflakes that silently glisten in the nook or cranny where we have landed. We keep busy contemplating some of life's most interesting issues.

Think of the beauty of the snow as it is silently falling all around you.

Perhaps the first snowfall of the year has come just as rush hour traffic begins.

It quickly becomes impossible to really enjoy the beauty of the snow with all the cars on the road and the necessity to keep your mind on your driving.

However, you can really appreciate the view when you are all by yourself gazing out the window or taking a walk in the winter wonderland outside. There is more time to contemplate everything in the quiet that surrounds you.

As you are thinking those deep thoughts, something may come to your mind that makes you smile. Sharing those thoughts with others may make them smile, too.

The great scientist Albert Einstein might have had intrapersonal intelligence. Many of Einstein's quotes indicate his deep thoughts about life.

For example:

"Everyone is a genius, but if you judge a fish on its ability to climb a tree, it will live it's whole life believing that it is stupid."

What he was telling us is the premise of this book.

We are, indeed, all smart! We are just smart in different ways!

What an interesting way Einstein chose to state that idea.

There are also examples in the Bible of people who probably had intrapersonal intelligence.

Elijah and John the Baptist seemed to spend much time by themselves and yet, at times, had a great following and the respect of those around them.

When King David was a little boy he spent many hours outside guarding the flocks of sheep.

It was quiet and he had a lot of time to think deep thoughts.

We know that David had at least one great friend in Saul's son, Jonathon. David's words in the book of Psalms would indicate that he spent a lot of time thinking about things. Many of those thoughts were about God.

Then, too, David is a perfect example of how God blesses us with more than just one intelligence. David loved the outdoors, spent time alone thinking, and was good at physical activities. He was also musical, and he certainly had a way with words.

These attributes indicate that David might have had strong, natural, intrapersonal, bodily-kinesthetic, musical, and verbal intelligence.

Some of these intelligences were more developed than others but God certainly had a special place for David to use each one of them.

The world needs deep thinkers like David to astonish, and motivate us all to do great things.

Remember the little boy in chapter seven who had mathematical-logical intelligence? I am sure that he spent a lot of time thinking about how that odd and even number, addition pattern worked before he could verbalize it to our class.

He enjoyed working by himself but he could also be a great friend.

Hopefully many of you learned about your special talent or ability at an early age and were able to easily fall into just the place God had for you.

Knowing that our lives have value and purpose can give great pleasure to the soul and a sense of contentment.

God truly has a special place for each of us.

Thank you Lord for the inspiring words that have come from the silent, sensitive snowflakes in this world.

THINK ABOUT

Mark 1:35 "Very early in the morning, while it was still dark, Jesus got up, left the house and went off to a solitary place, where he prayed."

Matthew 14:23 "And after he had dismissed the crowds, he went up on the mountain by himself to pray. When evening came, he was there alone . . ."

Luke 5:16 "So He Himself *often* withdrew into the wilderness and prayed."

1. Given the choice would you rather spend most of your time with friends or by yourself?

2. What activities do you enjoy doing all by yourself?

3. Which of your children or grandchildren tend to enjoy spending time by themselves? Think of things you can provide for them that will encourage their abilities.

CHAPTER THIRTEEN

"Outside Snowflakes" Natural Intelligence

You are probably thinking to yourself right now, "Outside Snowflakes?

Are there any other kind?"

When we think of snowflakes we are visualizing a beautiful outside scene and perhaps some snow-covered mountains.

Snowflakes fall outside! Everyone knows that! And people with natural intelligence love being outside!

Folks with this intelligence have a certain ability to easily identify things in nature. And when given the choice, they want to be out there enjoying it all. They can often find patterns and relationships in the things they see around them. Not only do these folks recognize plants, animals, and minerals, but also they may be able to classify them. People with natural intelligence learn best when they are outdoors.

Typical career interests or hobbies might include:

- park ranger
- scientist
- landscape architect
- biology teacher

- veterinarian
- botanist
- horticulturalist
- conservationist

Recently I met a woman at a store who found out that I was a teacher. She was worried about her grandchild who was spending most of her waking hours outside.

She told me how her granddaughter could name the trees by the leaves she found on the ground.

This child also knew the names of all the different birds that she saw sitting on the branches above her in her backyard and she was only 6 years old!

The grandmother and parents were concerned about her because she was struggling a bit with her reading skills. She preferred spending her time outside.

Now reading is very important but what an amazing intelligence this little girl had been given. How wonderful to discover it in one so young!

Her teacher and family can now use this information to teach her why it is important to learn how to read.

They can help her find special books and nature magazines that will catch her interest.

Using this knowledge will motivate her to learn to read about the things she loves.

This little girl will already have a head start in finding her special place in life.

In an earlier chapter I mentioned the people in our town that could always be found sitting outside visiting with their friends.

Every evening when I took my walk I would usually see those same groups of people.

The weather was lovely at that time of year and I often wondered why other people weren't outside enjoying the summer evening?

Then came fall and the weather turned chilly. These same people were still sitting outside visiting or playing basketball.

Then it dawned on me that these could be people with strong natural intelligence as well.

Perhaps these outside "snowflakes" were outside because they loved being outside.

Maybe they were not particularly fond of doing inside activities.

I imagine that they also enjoyed the company of other people who were part of the neighborhood get-togethers.

Dr. Gardner's research indicates that we have all of the 9 intelligences but are stronger in some than in others. So these people sitting outside on a lovely summer's evening could have been exhibiting natural as well as interpersonal intelligence.

I had to chuckle as I also noticed that all of these outside snowflakes had a camper sitting in their driveway or by the side of their house.

When you see a nature program on television you can't help but think that the people who plan and do these shows love nature. They love to see and do things that are outside. They make it look so interesting and beautiful.

I know of a young man who grew up on a farm. He really loved farming and thought of it as his future career.

With the economic situation and the reality of the problems that can be faced as a farmer, his parents wanted a different life for him. So they encouraged him to go into the ministry and sent him off to Bible school.

After graduation he got a job as a Children's Ministry Pastor.

With his winning smile and endearing ways he was such a blessing to the people of the church. They loved and appreciated him very much, especially the children.

However everyone who was around this young pastor for very long realized one thing—he longed to be doing things outside.

He loved mowing the church lawn and doing outside activities with the kids.

There was just something about working outside that appealed to him. You knew that farming or agricultural activities were always on his mind because he talked about them all the time.

After much prayer and wise advice from Godly mentors he eventually resigned his pastoral duties and went back to college to prepare for a career in agriculture. He still serves the Lord faithfully but now he knows where his true place of service is and God is using this young man in a mighty way.

In chapter one we learned how pressure from other ice crystals may influence the size and shape of snowflakes.

This young Pastor was under pressure from his parents to follow a different career path than farming. Their motives were good, but one of the best things we can do for our children is to pray for God's direction in their lives.

This young man will certainly serve the Lord much more happily by using the intelligences God has given him in the field of agriculture.

My favorite example of natural intelligence is a story about a young man who grew up on a small farm in Runnells, Iowa.

In the back of his boyhood home was a beautiful walnut woods full of interesting plants and animals. There was also a river nearby and an orchard with plenty of juicy apples.

He really enjoyed getting outside for a day of mushroom hunting, squirrel and pheasant hunting, or on a search for hickory nuts and walnuts.

As soon as his farm chores were done, he headed straight outside to play. Those hours he spent outdoors helped him become familiar with nature.

His parents sometimes worried about him when he didn't come home before dark. However they knew how much he enjoyed watching the beauty of the stars in the rural, Iowa sky.

No matter where he was, in the woods or down by the river, he could always find his way home.

Following graduation he entered the military and served in the army in the Pacific Theater during World War II.

During a particularly dangerous assignment, this young man's squad of men became lost, late at night, in the jungle.

They knew that if they could not make it back to their camp before the sun came up, they were in trouble.

There was a good possibility that they would be discovered by the enemy and taken prisoner or be shot and killed.

The squad leader did not know which direction would lead them safely back to their camp.

They were lost!

The young man quickly looked up into the night sky, noting the location of a certain star pattern. Within minutes, he was able to lead his fellow soldiers safely back to their camp.

All those evenings on that little farm back in Iowa, truly paid off for that young soldier and his brave friends who were far away from home . . . outside.

World War II Soldier Gazing at the Stars by Brett Crandel

THINK ABOUT

Psalm 8:3,4
"When I consider your heavens, the work of your fingers, the moon and the stars, which you have set in place what is mankind that you are mindful of them, human beings that you care for them? You have made them a little lower than the angels and crowned them with glory and honor. You made them rulers over the works of your hands; you put everything under their feet: all flocks and herds, and the animals of the wild, the birds in the sky, and the fish in the sea, all that swim the paths of the seas. Lord, our Lord, how majestic is your name in all the earth!

Genesis 1:14,15
"And God said, 'Let there be lights in the expanse of the heavens to separate the day from the night. And let them be for signs and for seasons, and for days and years, and let them be lights in the expanse of the heavens to give light upon the earth.' And it was so."

1. Given the choice, would you prefer spending time inside or outside?

2. What is your favorite outside activity?

3. What are some things that you do outside that might encourage others?

CHAPTER FOURTEEN

"Spiritual Snowflakes"
Existential or Spiritual Intelligence

In 1994 Dr. Howard Gardner followed up his original research with the possibility of one more intelligence.

This intelligence would be called existential or the intelligence of "big questions".

Other researchers became interested in the idea of spiritual or moral intelligence as well.

Individuals with existential (spiritual) intelligence enjoy questioning and thinking about life, death, and the ultimate realities of life.

They are characterized by a curiosity about why we are here on earth and where living things go when they die.

Famous people who might have had this intelligence were: Aristotle, Socrates, or Plato.

Billy Graham and Joel Osteen might be present day individuals with this intelligence.

People who are involved in ministry are usually blessed with this intelligence. They may have become interested in their profession because they were concerned about the eternal destiny of those around them. They believe that the Bible contains the answers to many of life's biggest questions.

It is my belief that God created each one of us with a certain amount of existential intelligence.

We cannot help but look around at all the amazing things we see and not wonder about who created them or what happens to people when they die.

At some time or another, we all ponder the deep questions of life.

Those who have a strong belief in God have the hope of eternal life in Heaven with a loving Father, the Creator of the universe. It gives us great comfort when the heavy snowstorms of life come our way.

And they always do!

Perhaps someone comes to your mind that is always concerned with the welfare of others and tries to be an encouragement to them.

They have been thinking about the real meaning of life and perhaps why they have been placed here on earth. They want to be of service to others.

Many pastors and missionaries show significant strengths in this intelligence.

Men and women like Billy Sunday, Dwight L. Moody, and Amy Carmichael have left our world with immeasurable contributions.

As a teenager our oldest son could usually be found at the back of the church after the services on Sunday morning.

He was not visiting with his teenage friends but he was back chatting it up with the older members of our congregation. He genuinely loved visiting with them and cared about how they were doing. You could see it in his eyes and hear it in his voice.

Our son would ask them about their activities that week and about their grandchildren. He was really listening to their responses.

He became a pastor and is now serving the Lord in a great church in Texas. Helping his congregation think about eternal things is the greatest desire of his life.

It is truly a blessing when we see this intelligence in young children.

Our oldest grandson thinks a lot about how he can help other people. He tries to be an encouragement to others in what he says and does.

I have watched him quietly slip off to help someone who is carrying a heavy load by going ahead of them to open the door.

Think about the times someone has done something like that for you and what an encouragement it has been.

Sometimes he will just go up to his Mom and tell her what a great job she is doing or ask how he might be able to help her.

He cannot stack three golf balls as quickly as his brother and people do not always notice his gift but what he does exhibits part of God's plan for his life.

Children and adults with this intelligence are a blessing to us all. They seem to have a special hope when facing life's challenges.

Many of you have an amazing faith in God that sustains you when things are going wrong. Your visible acts of faith encourage those around you.

Woman's Day magazine reported the results of a 2010 USA Today Gallup Poll. The article stated that 92% of Americans believe there is a God. That is quite a large percentage.

Perhaps that is because of the influence of the Godly people who began this nation over two hundred years ago.

Our national heritage is one of Godly beliefs. We saw it in the Pilgrims who came here looking for religious freedom to the steadfast faith of our founding fathers.

Contrary to what is being taught in many of our colleges these days, our Founding Fathers did write the Constitution of the United States with Godly principles in mind.

Perhaps that Godly national heritage is why 92% of Americans still today believe in the existence of God and 86% believe in the power of prayer.

In chapter one we talked about how the size and shape of a snowflake can be influenced by the ice crystals around it.

The influence of our Founding Fathers has certainly helped to shape who we are as a nation.

If you are an American citizen, you have grown up with the benefit of this national Godly influence.

Many of you have been blessed with spiritual intelligence. You think about the big questions of life and help those around you to think about them, too. Only time will tell the extent to which you will enlighten and encourage us all.

THINK ABOUT

II Corinthians 4:18 "So we fix our eyes not on what is seen, but on what is unseen, since what is seen is temporary, but what is unseen is eternal."

Romans 12:4-7 "For as we have many members in one body, and all members have not the same office: So we, being many, are one body in Christ, and every one members one of another. Having then gifts differing according to the grace that is given to us, whether prophecy, let us prophesy according to the proportion of faith; Or ministry, let us wait on our ministering: or he that teacheth, on teaching;"

Colossians 3:23, 24 "Whatever you do, work at it with all your heart, as working for the Lord, not for human masters, since you know that you will receive an inheritance from the Lord as a reward. It is the Lord Christ you are serving."

Philippians 4:8 "Finally, brothers, whatever is true, whatever is noble, whatever is right, whatever is pure, whatever is lovely, whatever is admirable—if anything is excellent or praiseworthy— think about such things."

Romans 14:18 ". . . because anyone who serves Christ in this way is pleasing to God and approved by men."

I Peter 2:12 "Live such good lives among the pagans that, though they accuse you of doing wrong, they may see your good deeds and glorify God on the day he visits us."

1. Who is someone in your life that helps you through the hard times? How do they help you?

2. Read a book or do research about Ruth Bell Graham, Billy Graham, or Billy Sunday. Why do you think they will be remembered as great spiritual leaders?

3. What is your favorite verse of encouragement in the Bible?

CHAPTER FIFTEEN

"Serious Snowflakes"
The First Born Child

The first beautiful snowflake that falls to earth catches our attention. It is inspiring and a natural born leader for all the other snowflakes to follow.

From the minute they were born, the first-born's parents hovered over them delighting in their first experience as parents.

Their parents read all the books and searched the Internet for the latest parenting and child-rearing research. They were particular about what their first-born did and who their friends were.

First-borns have more pictures in the family album than any other member of the family.

Their baby books contain detailed information on height, weight, eye color, and the delivering doctor's name.

Some first-borns are bossy but most are just wonderful leaders.

It is my opinion that some of this is because parents usually spend a lot of time telling their first born child to be responsible. They often place them in charge of their younger sibling(s).

As first-borns get older they may have more and more responsibility placed on their shoulders for those younger brothers and sisters.

My own Mom and Dad both worked full time. Because I was eight years older than my cute little sister, the task of babysitting occasionally fell upon me.

Sometimes I didn't mind that job and sometimes I just wanted to be with my friends or by myself. And in her defense, my dear, little sister did not always appreciate my "in charge" attitude.

When we reached adulthood it all got sorted out and we truly enjoy spending time with each other whenever we get a chance.

In the Old Testament we read the story of the life of Moses, a great leader of Israel.

Moses had an older sister and brother who struggled with the position in which God had placed their little brother. They questioned his leadership because, after all, they were his older brother and sister.

In Numbers 12 their bossiness got them into big-time trouble with the Lord.

Aaron and Miriam didn't like their little brother's choice for a wife and were probably jealous of many other facets of his life as well. They began to complain and their complaining got them into major trouble with God. Complaining often gets all of us into trouble.

Moses intervened with God on behalf of his brother and sister. However Miriam did become a leper for seven days and was forced to live outside the camp.

Many things we face in life affect who we become.

These things might include our heritage, the pressures of people around us, the events that transpire in our lives, and even our birth order.

Think about how you "fell" into your family.

Are you the oldest, the middle child, the baby of the family, or the lonely only?

Many years ago I picked up a copy of Dr. Kevin Leman's popular *Birth Order Book.*

Dr. Leman is an amazing author who gives us helpful, and often humorous, insight into our lives.

His books are a quick read because they are delightfully funny and jam-packed with wonderful stories that illustrate his points.

Just the titles are enough to make you burst out laughing right there in the bookstore.

One very popular book about child rearing is called *How to Make Your Child Mind Without Losing Yours.*

I am told that Dr. Leman was once on a well-known talk show and went out into the audience asking several quick questions of different individuals. He had never met these people and knew very little about them but he correctly guessed their birth order.

We also know that adoptions, blended families, or the death of a sibling can affect the characteristics of traditional birth order roles.

On one occasion we met a young teen that was helping to get everyone organized into a zip-line activity at Camp Chautauqua, a Christian camp in Miamisburg, Ohio.

She was doing a wonderful job and seemed like a natural born leader. The kids around her were benefitting from her great help that day.

I assumed that she might be a first-born child.

When I asked her, she told me that she was not the first-born but the baby of the family.

After further conversation with her, she revealed that she had an older sister who was in her late 20's.

That age gap of over 15 years had given this younger girl a chance to assume first-born characteristics as well as those of the youngest child. She loved being with all the kids, having fun outside, and they enjoyed her leadership.

Information about birth order can help us understand why people act or speak the way they do in certain situations.

It can also help us be more aware of our own strengths and weaknesses so that we can fall perfectly into place in God's plan for our lives.

Newscasters, TV talk show hosts, and airline pilots tend to be first-born or only children.

Prominent examples include: Walter Cronkite, Peter Jennings, Dan Rather, Ted Koppel, Oprah, Donahue, Geraldo, Arsenio Hall, Rush Limbaugh, and retired airline captain, Chesley Sullenberger III (The hero of the Hudson).

A majority of the United States Presidents were either the oldest child or the oldest boy in their family.

All but two of the first astronauts sent into space were first-borns, and the other two were "only children".

Generally speaking the first-born boy and the first-born girl in most families are natural leaders. They also tend to be conscientious and reliable.

Some are perfectionists who don't like surprises.

Although firstborns are typically assertive, many are also confirmed people pleasers. They try to be model children and may have a strong need for approval from anyone in authority.

Only children are often firstborns time ten. They are even more responsible and even bigger perfectionists and usually get along better with people older than themselves. After all, they spend the majority of their time with older people!

Because each birth order is different, they each face different issues and concerns.

Our daughter-in-law is an only child and she remembers being worried about what might happen to her if her mother and father both died.

If you were not an only child you probably wouldn't think about those things. Now that you are aware of that you will know what kinds of things to share with your only child that will encourage them and assuage their fears.

Every birth order has its own delightful and not so delightful characteristics.

As a teacher I had a few classes that just seemed to have more problems than others in getting along with one another.

Using birth order information would sometimes help me figure out how to manage the class and what kind of speech to give when they needed it.

This information can help you manage your family situations as well.

When I first discovered birth order characteristics I was having a rather rocky start with this one class.

Other people who worked with them also noticed that they had a hard time working together in a group.

Finally I had had enough arguing, bossiness, and pouting.

I asked the children to raise their hands if they were the oldest child in their family or the oldest boy or girl. Almost every hand in the classroom went up.

They were all struggling with trying to be the leader. They were telling everyone else what to do and it was obviously not working.

The next step was a class meeting in the back of the room for "THE SPEECH".

I told them that someday they might all be wonderful leaders of companies, or churches, or organizations and that we would be so proud of them.

At some time that year I would call on them to help lead groups in our room.

I reminded them that they were all natural born leaders and God had given them that special ability.

I hoped that they would use their gift wisely in whatever position God called them to serve.

These students saw things that needed to be done and they usually knew how to get it done quickly and efficiently.

Not everyone is born with that wonderful gift.

They were challenged throughout the year to use their birth order wisely because with leadership comes great responsibility.

Natural born leaders must strive to help the people they lead by letting them know why something needs to be done.

We all work together better when we understand the importance of the job or the reason for doing it in a certain way.

Finally I let this wonderful class know that God is ultimately in control. He had placed me, as their teacher in the classroom, to be responsible for their welfare that year.

The speech worked pretty well and it took the pressure off for some of them.

That year I didn't forget too many important details because I had a lot of first-born helpers giving me great, timely advice!

When they all learned how reassuring it is to know that God is really in control, the atmosphere in the class became more relaxed.

If things went wrong in our class, we made corrections and remembered that, through it all, God would take care of us.

This gift of leadership can also be found in situations where the first-born might be a boy and the next child a girl.

The oldest girl could quite possibly exhibit the same qualities of leadership as her older brother.

Our youngest son has many of the characteristics of the youngest child. However, because there is more than a 5-year span between he and his older sister, he also has first-born characteristics.

When our two older children moved out of our home, this youngest child was also the only child for many years. He has an interesting mix of oldest, only, and last child characteristics.

Perhaps you know someone like this, too. When we use this information about birth order it can help us understand many things about the people in our lives.

Throughout history God has given us some great first-born leaders.

George Washington led a struggling young country when they needed it most.

Washington assumed the characteristics of a first-born because there was a span of over five years between he and his older brother Lawrence.

First-born Abraham Lincoln led our country with determination and love throughout the days of a terrifying Civil War.

Sir Winston Churchill, the leader of Great Britain during World War II, was a first-born child. He had a speech impediment and failed his college entrance test three times but he became a soldier/journalist and artist.

Churchill inspired the world to fight against the evils of Adolph Hitler's Nazi Germany.

We thank the Lord for those serious, first-born Snowflakes.

Their special kind of sparkle leads the way for us all.

THINK ABOUT

Matthew 20:26 "But among you it will be different. Whoever wants to be a leader among you must be your servant."

Galatians 6:9 " Let us not become weary in doing good, for at the proper time we will reap a harvest if we do not give up."

Philippians 2:3-7
"Do nothing out of selfish ambition or vain conceit. Rather, in humility value others above yourselves, not looking to your own interests but each of you to the interests of the others. In your relationships with one another, have the same mindset as Christ Jesus: Who, being in very nature God, did not consider equality with God something to be used to his own advantage; rather, he made himself nothing by taking the very nature of a servant, being made in human likeness.

Mark 10:44,45
". . . and whoever wants to be first must be slave of all. For even the Son of Man did not come to be served, but to serve, and to give his life as a ransom for many."

1. Write a letter to your oldest child or grandchild telling them what you admire about them. Encourage them to

use their talents for the Lord and tell them that you are praying for them.

2. Make a list of the people in your life that you consider good leaders. What do you appreciate about the way they lead?

3. Good leaders look for the strengths in those that they are leading and try to lead by example. Does this kind of leadership style characterize your life?

CHAPTER SIXTEEN

"Second Snowflakes"
The Middle Child

So we have all marveled over that first snowflake.

We looked at it under a magnifying lens and drew pictures of it.

The teacher showed us how to make one out of paper.

We copied a poem about it and placed it on the hallway wall for everyone to see.

The next day it snowed again.

"That's nice," we all said. "Now let's get back to work."

The more the snow fell during the winter, the less we really noticed it. At least that's true for the most part here in Iowa.

"You've seen one snowflake, you've seen them all," some would say.

Sometimes we just got sick and tired of seeing the snow coming down.

We knew what it was going to be like trying to drive our car home through the slush and ice a little later in the day.

Some of us probably had to get out and shovel the stuff so that we could just get our cars into the garage.

The second and third snowfalls are obviously not as highly regarded as that first beautiful snowflake of the season.

That gives you a little taste of how middle children must feel at times.

As the middle child you might have wondered about your place in life or worried about how you would ever live up to your older brother or sister's talents.

Occasionally people you know and love may have pointed out your lack of ability in the light of the behaviors or gifts they noticed in your siblings.

Don't go there middle children!

God has uniquely made you with a special position in your family. You have fallen into that special, middle place. God loves you very much and He has given you different talents and abilities that will help you find your own wonderful place in life.

In the last chapter we talked about how the first-born child sometimes becomes a marvelous leader. However the Bible is full of middle and youngest children who were also used by God. This list would include Isaac, Jacob, Joseph, Moses, and David.

Some middle children were listed by name in the Bible and we never hear them mentioned again.

Be sure that you do not overlook the middle children in your life. These dear people may be exhibiting quite different intelligences from their older brother or sister.

Also, busy parents often don't think about the place of the middle child in their family.

That wonderful middle child will usually be your peacemaker but they want you to notice them, too, so they may "act out" a bit in order to get your attention.

If you take the time to explain to them about how God has uniquely created each one of us, it will really help them find their own special place.

Remind them that you can hardly wait to see what their special gifts from God will be. Complement them for their unique differences.

The following famous Americans were middle children: John F. Kennedy, George H.W. Bush, Richard Nixon, Donald Trump, and Marie Osmond.

You "second snowflakes" are usually good at negotiating and may have what many would call "people skills".

Good career choices for middle children might be healthcare, law enforcement, firefighting, construction, or teaching.

Experts on birth order tell us that some middle children may be "hard to read".

They want to be different from their older siblings, which may show itself in a variety of ways.

Middle children often desire the attention received by the older child and envy how their younger brother or sister escapes punishment for breaking the rules.

They can be secretive or have a hard time sharing their true feelings.

If a middle child does not feel that they have a special place in their family they may reach out to friends for acceptance. Sometimes that is a good thing and sometimes it is not.

Middle children seem to have a way of understanding how others are feeling and easily become the peacemakers of their group. Their position in the middle provides much practice and eventually expertise in settling the arguments between older and younger brothers and sisters.

These "second snowflakes" can be very independent and very creative.

Although not desiring the role of a leader, they may become quite good as entrepreneurs or negotiators.

Don't be surprised if your middle child doesn't quickly return your E-mail, text messages, or phone calls. It might seem to take forever for them to check their voicemail. It doesn't mean that they are upset about something or angry with you. They just often forget to communicate with others. Middle children are not very concerned about communication. It doesn't seem to be high on their list of things to do.

When you learn about these characteristics of middle children it can help you begin to realize why your sibling or friends act the way they do. These folks just don't think about communication like the rest of us.

Then there is the matter of keeping the peace. Middle children typically don't like it when people are arguing. They really don't want to be involved in situations where people are upset with each other. It makes sense that after spending years living between older and younger siblings, middle children just want everyone to get along.

You wonderful second snowflakes are definitely peacemakers.

The years that I had my very best classes were years when much was accomplished because everyone seemed to be on the same wavelength. No individual student really stood out. They just all worked together and did their best.

One of those classes was very dear to my heart.

Using the same strategy I had in the past, I asked the students to raise their hands if they were the middle child in their family.

Almost every hand in the classroom went up.

It was a pleasure to teach this class. I didn't have to spend much time that year settling arguments in the classroom or on the playground.

The children worked well together in groups or by themselves.

They did not argue about who was going to do what or how it should be done. Everything was calmly discussed, plans were made, and work was completed. No wonder I loved this class so much!

Because middle children try their best to get along, they might struggle at times with frustration. Instead of confronting situations or people, they may find themselves ignoring things that bother them in an attempt to keep the peace.

Our lovely middle snowflake reminded me of an important Biblical truth several years ago: "Speak the truth in love."

She has helped me to learn that frustration is not a good thing and can build to serious levels if left unattended. Sometimes we just need to let folks know how their words or actions make us feel.

Our daughter enjoys the friendship of many dear friends because she knows when confrontation is necessary and when the situation just needs to be dropped.

We can all benefit from that sparkling snowflake of scriptural wisdom.

Yes, the snowflakes of the midwinter season often fall unnoticed by the world.

They don't get as much attention as those first, amazing snowflakes of the year.

The second snowflakes also fall much more silently than the windy blast of the blizzard.

Nevertheless, our middle children are also blessed with very special gifts.

Spending time with them can be a delightful, relaxing experience.

They help us all get along together in this life.

"Blessed are the Peacemakers!"

THINK ABOUT

Hebrews 12:14
"Pursue peace with all people, and holiness, without which no one will see the Lord."

Matthew 5:9
"Blessed are the peacemakers, for they will be called sons of God."

Ephesians 4:3
"Make every effort to keep the unity of the Spirit through the bond of peace."

Romans 14:19
"Let us therefore make every effort to do what leads to peace and to mutual edification."

1. Write a letter to your middle child (children) or grandchildren telling them what you admire about them. Encourage them to use their talents for the Lord and tell them that you are praying for them.

2. If you are a middle child think about a time when you have helped to settle an argument. What might have happened if you had not been able to help?

3. If you are a middle child, how are your talents different from your older and younger sibling(s)?

CHAPTER SEVENTEEN

"Blizzards"
The Last-born Child

If you have a last-born child you probably know why I have entitled this chapter "Blizzards".

The last-born child is the blizzard. They usually love being the life of the party and there is always a flurry of excitement when they are around.

It is hard to ignore a blizzard. They usually demand your attention.

During a blizzard in Iowa, the school superintendent would be listening for the latest weather forecast. That forecast would generally determine whether to cancel classes for the day or dismiss classes early.

The children were delighted when a "Snow Day" was declared and we, too, are usually delighted with the antics of the last-born blizzard.

They are the clowns of the family and love to keep us all entertained. Sometimes it is because this is the only way that the youngest child can capture the attention away from older brothers and sisters.

Our Ohio granddaughter cracks us all up with her unusual and hilarious pictures. She is learning to make her own mark on the world and it is definitely different from that of her two older brothers.

The youngest can delight us with crazy stories, funny dance moves, and sometimes some pretty scary schemes.

Blizzards, however, can be costly in a community. Snowplows, de-icing chemicals, power outages, increased heating costs and traffic jam inconveniences all add up.

Costly financial problems can also happen if a last-born child becomes irresponsible with their spending habits or if their daredevil plans go awry. They just want to have a good time and sometimes don't think about what it may cost.

The youngest child can enjoy being the life of the party. They learn to develop comedic skills in order to upstage their older siblings and it usually works pretty well.

Some of the world's most famous comedians are last-born children.

These folks have made a name for themselves by keeping others entertained. And who doesn't need a good laugh as we go through life. Being able to make others laugh or smile is a wonderful gift from God.

Many last-born individuals find great satisfaction and success in sales and vocations that involve high interactions with others.

Sometimes when I am in stores shopping I will notice a very good salesman. They will usually be outgoing and very familiar with their product. These are the kind of salespeople that come right up to you with a friendly manner and happy face. They can talk your socks off about their amazing product and why you should buy it.

When you ask them if they are the youngest in their family, it is always interesting to see their astonishment at your accurate prediction.

Be sure to remind them that they have probably chosen a good career and tell them what a great job they are doing.

Knowing information like this about your children can be helpful in guiding them towards important career choices.

Artistic career choices such as acting are also very appealing to the last-born child. They may excel at more public roles where they can gain attention in a variety of important ways.

The last-born child will probably at age 40, with many outstanding accomplishments in life, still be referred to by their nickname.

I had to laugh out loud as I thought of our own youngest child who is now grown and is still sometimes called "Mikey" by those who know and love him!

What a wonderful young man he has become and God has used his last-born qualities and skills in many ways.

Information about birth order characteristics is a great way to gain insight into the lives of the children and people who are dear to you.

As more snowflakes fall into our family we become more confident of our snowflake parenting skills and relax a little.

Maybe that is why the last-born child behaves the way they do.

Parents often tend to let the youngest child get away with more than the first born or middle children.

It is important to repeat that birth order characteristics do not always fit every situation. Many other things can have an impact on who we are and what we become.

A lady I once visited with told me that she was the youngest child in her family. I would not have guessed that from what I knew about her and what she did.

This dear lady was the youngest of three girls. Her older sisters were constantly striving with each other for attention from the parents.

The middle sister had talents that were more obvious than those of her older sister. Those two older girls were enveloped in a struggle to win parental approval and the youngest sister just sat back and tried to keep the peace.

Watch out for those last snowflakes, however. They are often risk takers and will fall where other flakes have not been brave enough to go.

It may also cause your first-born and middle child to become resentful of the last-born child. They could become disrespectful of your parenting skills if they see you allowing the youngest to break the rules.

Make sure that the people around you know how special and different they are.

Let them know you are excited to help them discover the talents that God has given them. And remember that some talents are easier to measure and see.

You really need to be alert if you want to help the people you love find their special place in life.

In the years when my classroom needed lots of direction and upkeep I discovered what you might have already suspected. These classes were full of last-born children.

We enjoyed a special kind of humor that they brought to the classroom with their crazy antics and stories.

They loved to act out stories and were not afraid to work their blizzard magic in front of the entire class.

I had to be careful when administering discipline because they were very good at talking themselves out of trouble and were quite hilarious while doing it.

When King David was a young man his parents and older brothers often left him to his own devices while he was out taking care of the sheep. He seemed to have little fear when a lion or a bear approached his flock.

Perhaps as the youngest child he just didn't stop to think about the danger he was facing. Possibly the excitement of trying out his little sling overcame his common sense.

Once David was sent to check on his older brothers, who were soldiers for King Saul. They could not understand their little brother's bravery in the face of such giant danger.

Because of David's fearless nature and God's help, he was able to defeat a giant and eventually became the King of Israel. God had an important job for this youngest son of Jesse.

Help the little blizzards you know learn to follow the rules so that they will not do something foolish.

Try to be a consistent parent or teacher because the older snowflakes will be watching.

Blizzards can cause a great deal of commotion but they are also breath-taking!

And sometimes a "Snow Day" is just what we all need!

Evan

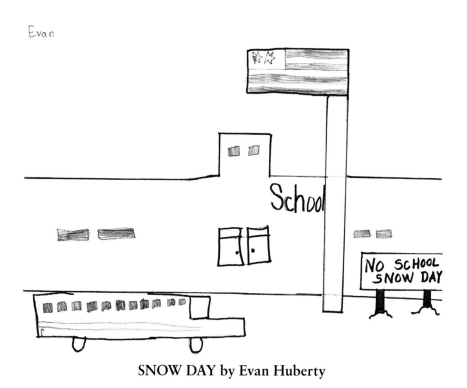

SNOW DAY by Evan Huberty

THINK ABOUT

I Timothy 4:12
"Don't let anyone look down on you because you are young, but set an example for the believers in speech, in conduct, in love, in faith and in purity."

Genesis 37:2; 39:1-4 "These are the generations of Jacob. Joseph, being seventeen years old, was pasturing the flock with his brothers. He was a boy . . . And Joseph brought a bad report of them to their father . . . Now Joseph had been brought down to Egypt, and Potiphar, an officer of Pharaoh, the captain of the guard, an Egyptian, had bought him from the Ishmaelites who had brought him down there. The LORD was with Joseph, and he became a successful man, and he was in the house of his Egyptian master. His master saw that the LORD was with him and that the LORD caused all that he did to succeed in his hands. So Joseph found favor in his sight and attended him, and he made him overseer of his house and put him in charge of all that he had."

1. Take time today to talk with your youngest child or grandchild. Ask them to tell you about the things they like to do. Find out what their favorite activities or interests are.

2. Ask your youngest child to tell you what they think their older brother(s) or sister(s) are good at doing. Remind them that God has given each of us special talents.

3. Write a letter to your youngest child or grandchild telling them what you admire about them. Encourage them to use their talents for the Lord and tell them that you are praying for them.

CHAPTER EIGHTEEN

"Snowflake Summary"

Scientists tell us that there are no two snowflakes exactly alike.

That is a powerful thought when you think of all the snowflakes that fall to earth! And, in my opinion, it definitely points to the creation of our world by a higher being.

Like beautiful snowflakes we too are uniquely created by a loving, Heavenly Father who made us all with special skills (intelligences) and placed us within our families in a certain order. There are no two of us exactly alike.

Some of our talents are easy to see and measure. After being tested at school, occasionally a child will be labeled as "gifted". Strength in language arts, math, sports, and music areas are quickly noticed.

When a young person does not seem to have strong skills in these areas, they may feel that they are not intelligent.

They may give up because they feel that they have nothing wonderful to offer to the world.

It is very easy for young people to get down on themselves when they are compared with one of their siblings or friends at school who have more visible talents.

No matter our age we all want to know that we have something special to offer. We want to leave behind a legacy and make our mark on this world.

There are too many people who have no idea what their real gifts are and wind up choosing careers that may not lead where God had intended.

After reading this book it is my hope that you will be looking for strengths in the lives of those around you as well as in your own life.

Encourage the people around you by letting them know what you notice.

Sadly, I recently learned of a mentally challenged young man whose mother purchased many wonderful gifts for her other children on their birthdays.

For this son, however, she would send a card with a garbage bag inside.

It was her way of indicating what she thought this child was. Garbage!

I do not know him personally but what a terrible agony I felt for him.

That young man is full of wonderful potential. It is my prayer that other people will come along side him and help him see his amazing gifts.

For whatever reasons, that disturbed and hurtful mother does not have any idea of what a wonderful blessing her son is to those who may choose to be part of his life.

Our words and actions towards our children are powerful and can have a direct affect on what they become.

We need to remind our children that a loving Heavenly Father has uniquely created us all.

Teach those who are dear to you that their intelligences are sometimes easy to spot and sometimes may take several years to become obvious.

People, like snowflakes, can change under pressure.

Comments or observations from those around us can have a powerful influence on what we do with our lives.

Also, like snowflakes, we change with age. As we mature we may develop an intelligence that we did not really use as younger snowflakes.

How wonderful it is to keep learning and trying new things.

Abraham Lincoln tried and failed to attain public office many times before eventually becoming a great leader of our country.

Some snowflakes stick around for a long time and some melt away too soon.

They are like the people we know who may live for a very long time, or die way too young from accidents or terrible diseases.

Some snowflakes fall gently and silently upon the earth and some arrive in the mighty blast of a blizzard.

People come to this earth in a certain order in their families. We do not choose our birth order but it certainly has some affect on what we become.

Our many different intelligences and our birth order obviously help to determine who we are and what we can accomplishment on this earth.

Having a better understanding of intelligences and birth order may have a wonderful bearing on our earthly accomplishments and the legacy that we will leave.

Children need to be taught that they are unique.

They should not compare themselves to others in an unfavorable light nor should we.

When children become acquainted with Gardner's multiple intelligences and learn their own strengths, they tend to build self-esteem. Then they can learn to rely on those who have intelligences that are stronger than their own. They can use that knowledge to work together and benefit everyone.

The classroom communities that are built on this kind of knowledge function much more smoothly and efficiently than traditional classrooms.

There are too many people who have never had the benefit of the snowflake lessons, nor did their parents.

Some situations are extremely sad and we can only thank the Lord for His graciousness to us.

Some of you may be snowflakes that never knew how much you sparkled.

Hopefully the information from this book will have been helpful to you. Have fun developing your newfound talents. It is never too late.

Use these lessons from the snowflake to find your special place of service. Then take what you have learned and help someone else as well.

Teach your children and grandchildren the lessons of the snowflake.

Help those who are dear to you learn to sparkle while they are here on this earth.

It is so inspiring to look out your window on a lovely winter day and see those sparkling snowflakes falling into place.

THINK ABOUT

Jeremiah 1: 5
"Before I formed you in the womb I knew you, before you were born I set you apart;"

Psalm 139:14
"I will praise thee; for I am fearfully and wonderfully made: marvelous are thy works; and that my soul knoweth right well."

Job 37:14 . . . "Stop and consider the wondrous works of God."

I Peter 4:10
"Each one should use whatever gift he has received to serve others, faithfully administering God's grace in its various forms."

ACKNOWLEDGEMENTS

Research by Dr. Howard Gardner

Research by Dr. Kevin Leman

Research by Dr. Alfred Adler

Snowflake Bentley by Jacquelin Briggs Martin, Illustrated by Mary Azarian

Gifts that are evident in the lives of my husband, children, and grandchildren

Inspiring events from the lives of my students at Des Moines Christian School

People in our local Iowa community of Altoona, Iowa

Dr. Bob Stouffer, Superintendent at Des Moines Christian School

Elementary Art Department at DMCS—Student Drawings

My father, Max Perryman, who was the World War II soldier in Chapter 13

WEBSITES:

The following websites may be used to take a multiple intelligence test and find your own strongest intelligences:

http://www.bgfl.org/custom/resources_ftp/client_ftp/ks3/ict/multiple_int/questions/choose_lang.cfm

www.literacyworks.org/mi/assessment/findyourstrengths.html

CPSIA information can be obtained at www.ICGtesting.com
Printed in the USA
LVOW132317290513

335980LV00004B/11/P